Artificial Intelligence

7

Textbook

(As per CBSE Syllabus Code 417)

Harmeet Kaur
M. Anhitha

bpb
www.bpbonline.com

FIRST EDITION 2021

REPRINT 2023

ISBN: 978-93-90684-083

LIMITS OF LIABILITY AND DISCLAIMER OF WARRANTY

The information contained in this book is true to correct and the best of author's and publisher's knowledge. The author has made every effort to ensure the accuracy of these publications, but publisher cannot be held responsible for any loss or damage arising from any information in this book.

All trademarks referred to in the book are acknowledged as properties of their respective owners but BPB Publications cannot guarantee the accuracy of this information.

CBSE is no way connected with this book. This Book is written solely for the benefit and guidance for CBSE examination.

Distributors:

BPB PUBLICATIONS

20, Ansari Road, Darya Ganj

New Delhi-110002

Ph: 23254990/23254991

DECCAN AGENCIES

4-3-329, Bank Street,

Hyderabad-500195

Ph: 24756967/24756400

MICRO MEDIA

Shop No. 5, Mahendra Chambers,

150 DN Rd. Next to Capital Cinema,

V.T. (C.S.T.) Station, MUMBAI-400 001

Ph: 22078296/22078297

BPB BOOK CENTRE

376 Old Lajpat Rai Market,

Delhi-110006

Ph: 23861747

To View Complete
BPB Publications Catalogue
Scan the QR Code:

Published by Manish Jain for BPB Publications, 20 Ansari Road, Darya Ganj, New Delhi-110002 and Printed at Manipal Technologies Ltd., Karnataka (India)

www.bpbonline.com

Dedicated to

Our parents, family members,
peers & dear students.

About the Authors

Harmeet Kaur is currently working as Senior Computer Teacher, Department of Computer Science at Heritage Xperiential Learning School, Gurugram. She has over 21 years of experience in the field of education; teaching Computer Science, Informatics Practices and Multimedia and Web Technologies to grades XI and XII along with a background of mentoring, IT curriculum development for STEM integration, and staff training and development. She has led various in-house projects such as Learning Management System to propagate collaborative personalized e-Learning. She is well adept in Google Apps for Education and uses it as a primary platform for her classroom teaching. She integrates multiple teaching styles to build digital literacy skills in millennial learners while strongly promoting safe and ethical use of technology. She believes in driving the experiential and project-based pedagogy by imparting mobile computing skills to high school students. She has conducted various workshops in and around Delhi-NCR to train teachers with latest pedagogies of classroom management, incorporating Tech to teach STEM education and “learning by doing” hands-on workshops. She has authored training material for in-house teacher training and been constructive in ICT curriculum development.

LinkedIn: linkedin.com/in/harmeetkaur2504

Website: www.harmeetkaur.in

M. Anhitha has an overall professional experience of more than 9 years. She has written many books including Fundamentals of computer science, Information Technology and currently working as a writer in computer science where she collaborates and works with enthusiasts across the globe. She has done B.Tech in Information Technology and M.Tech in Computer Science. She likes to keep herself updated to the latest trends and technologies.

LinkedIn: linkedin.com/in/m-anhitha-234130206

Blog: https://taartech.blogspot.com/

Acknowledgements

We would like to express our gratitude to everyone at BPB Publications for giving us this opportunity to write the book. We are thankful to all the resource persons at BPB Publications for editing, technical reviewing and language editing the book.

We are thankful to each other and our families for being supportive in numerous ways and for giving their unconditional love and support at all times.

Lastly, but not the least, we would like to thank God for bearing us with courage and humility to be able to write this book for our students.

— Harmeet Kaur

— M. Anhitha

Preface

Artificial intelligence (AI) studies human behaviour and creates a machines that can demonstrate human like behaviours (learn, plan and solve problems) with minimal human interference. AI has been a vast subject which focuses on some of the major topics such as automation, computer vision, facial recognition systems, game artificial intelligence, hybrid intelligent system, problem solving, machine learning, and natural language understanding and so on.

This book is divided into three chapters and provides a detailed description of the basic concepts of Artificial Intelligence.

Chapter 1 explains what is Artificial Intelligence, its applications in their daily lives. Further it explains three domains of Artificial Intelligence, Domains of AI, how Data for Artificial Intelligence, Natural Language Processing, and Computer Vision is related.

Chapter 2 provides the detail explanation of Skills required for AI ready future job, AI applications by using the Research template and the ethical concerns of AI You will know how AI has been affecting jobs in various industries and the home communication and collaborative skills to design activities

Chapter 3 focuses on the complexities of concepts surrounding ethics (bias, access, privacy) in AI. Further the emerging trends in different fields which are getting affected by AI is explained.

Throughout the book many activities have been given in the chapter to understand the concept in a better way.

Sample project has been given which explains the creation of ChatBot using Pictoblox.

One sample paper with solutions has been given to practice.

Key terms in the form of glossary have been given to enhance the learning.

Syllabus for Middle School (class VI/VII/VIII)

INTRODUCTION TO ARTIFICIAL INTELLIGENCE

OBJECTIVES OF THE MODULE:

This module of Artificial Intelligence focuses on:

- Helping learners understand the world of Artificial Intelligence and its applications through games, activities, and multi-sensorial learning to become AI-Ready.
- Allowing the learners to construct the meaning of AI through interactive participation and engaging hands-on activities.

OUTLINE CURRICULUM:

MODULE	SUB-UNIT	DURATION
Introduction to Artificial Intelligence	Excite	2.5 Hours
	Relate	02 Hours
	Purpose	02 Hours
	Possibilities	02 Hours
	AI Ethics	3.5 Hours
TOTAL DURATION		**12 hours**
TOTAL MARKS		**50 marks (Theory = 15 + Practical 35)**

DETAILED CURRICULUM:

SUB-UNIT	LEARNING OUTCOMES	SESSION / ACTIVITY / PRACTICAL
1. EXCITE	• To identify and appreciate Artificial Intelligence and describe its applications in daily life.	Session: Introduction to AI and setting up the context of the curriculum
		Ice Breaker Activity: Dream Smart Home idea Learners to design a rough layout of floor plan of their dream smart home.
	• To relate, apply and reflect on the Human-Machine Interactions. • To identify and interact with the three domains of AI: Data, Computer Vision and Natural Language Processing.	Recommended Activity: The AI Game Learners' to participate in three games based on different AI domains. • Game 1: Rock, Paper and Scissors (based on data) • Game 2: Mystery Animal (based on Natural Language Processing - NLP) • Game 3: Emoji Scavenger Hunt (based on Computer Vision - CV)

	• To undergo an assessment for analysing progress towards acquired AI-Readiness skills.	Recommended Activity: AI Quiz (Paper Pen/Online Quiz)
	• To imagine, examine and reflect on the skills required for futuristic job opportunities.	Recommended Activity: Writing a Letter to one's future self Learners to write a letter to self-keeping the future in context. They will describe what they have learnt so far or what they would like to learn someday
2. RELATE	• Learners' to relate to application of Artificial Intelligence in their daily lives	Video Session: To watch a video Introducing the concept of Smart Cities, Smart Schools and Smart Homes
	• To unleash their imagination towards smart homes and build an interactive story around it. • To relate, apply and reflect on the Human–Machine interactions.	Recommended Activity: Write an Interactive Story Learners' to draw a floor plan of a Home/ School/ City and write an interactive story around it using the Story Speaker extension in Google docs.
3. PURPOSE	• To understand the impact of Artificial Intelligence on Sustainable Development Goals to develop responsible citizenship.	Session: Introduction to UN Sustainable Development Goals
		Recommended Activity: Go Goals Board Game Learners to answer questions on Sustainable Development Goals
4. POSSIBILITIES	• To research and develop awareness of skills required for jobs of the future. • To imagine, examine and reflect on the skills required for the futuristic opportunities. • To develop effective communication and collaborative work skills.	Session: Theme-based research and Case Studies Learners will listen to various case-studies of inspiring start-ups, companies or communities where AI has been involved in real-life. Learners will be allotted a theme around which they need to search for present AI trends and have to visualise the future of AI in and around their respective theme.
		Recommended Activity: Job Ad Creating activity Learners to create a job advertisement for a firm describing the nature of job available and the skill-set required for it 10 years down the line. They need to figure out how AI is going to transform the nature of jobs and create the Ad accordingly.

5. AI ETHICS	• To understand and reflect on the ethical issues around AI.	Video Session: Discussing about AI Ethics Recommended Activity: Ethics Awareness Students play the role of major stakeholders and they have to decide what is ethical and what is not for a given scenario.
	• To gain awareness around AI bias and AI access.	Session: AI Bias and AI Access • Discussing about the possible bias in data collection • Discussing about the implications of AI technology
	• To let the students analyse the advantages and disadvantages of Artificial Intelligence.	Recommended Activity: Balloon Debate Students divide in teams of 3 and 2 teams are given the same theme. One team goes in affirmation to AI for their section while the other one goes against it. They have to come up with their points as to why AI is beneficial/ harmful for the society.

Contents

1 INTRODUCTION TO ARTIFICIAL INTELLIGENCE

Structure Bot

In this chapter, we will discuss:

- The meaning of the term Artificial Intelligence
- Applications of Artificial Intelligence
- Three domains of Artificial Intelligence

Objective Bot

At the end of this chapter, you should be able to:

- Know the use of AI domains in various applications
- Learn to relate Data for Artificial Intelligence, Natural Language Processing, and Computer Vision
- Understand the applications of Natural Language Processing, and Computer Vision

Introduction to Artificial Intelligence

Artificial Intelligence, or 'AI', is the technological innovation for all the new age changes which are happening all around us.

Artificial intelligence (AI) is an intelligence which is demonstrated by machines, and not the natural intelligence which is shown or displayed by humans and animals. The term "*Artificial Intelligence*" is often used to describe machines (or computers) which mimic the "*cognitive*" functions that humans associate with the human mind, such as "*learning*" and "*problem solving*".

A quip in Tesler's Theorem says "*AI is whatever hasn't been done yet.*"

Modern machine capabilities explain that AI include successfully in:

- Understanding human speech
- Competing at the highest level in strategic game systems (chess)
- Automatically operating cars
- Intelligent routing in content delivery networks
- Military simulations

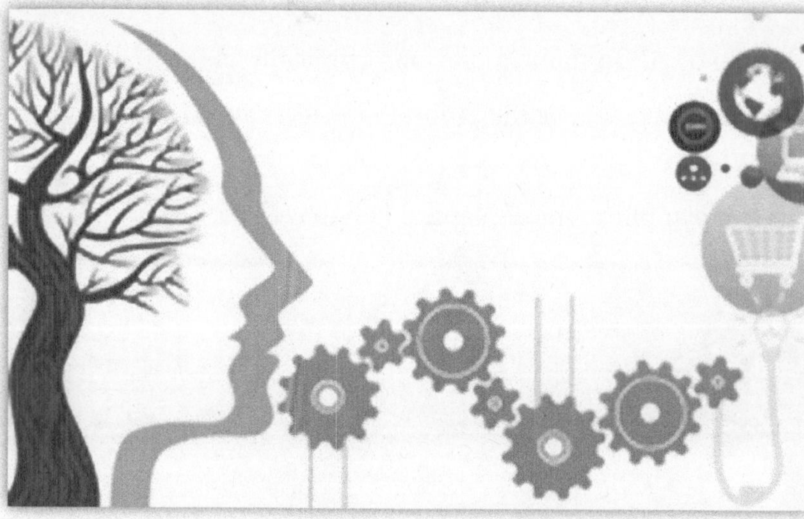

Fact Bot

AI pets are robots that look, feel, and act like a real animal. It is expected that AI-driven pets will be widely available in the market by 2025.

Activity I

Talk to Eliza, first chatbots created in 1964

How it works:

- The chatbot works by typing something and it will give you a reply.
- The replies are somewhat limited; however, it is still fun and safe to chat with it. Because of this, it is highly recommended for children who are still learning how to read and write.

1. Go to the link: https://www.masswerk.at/eliza/
2. The following screen appear:

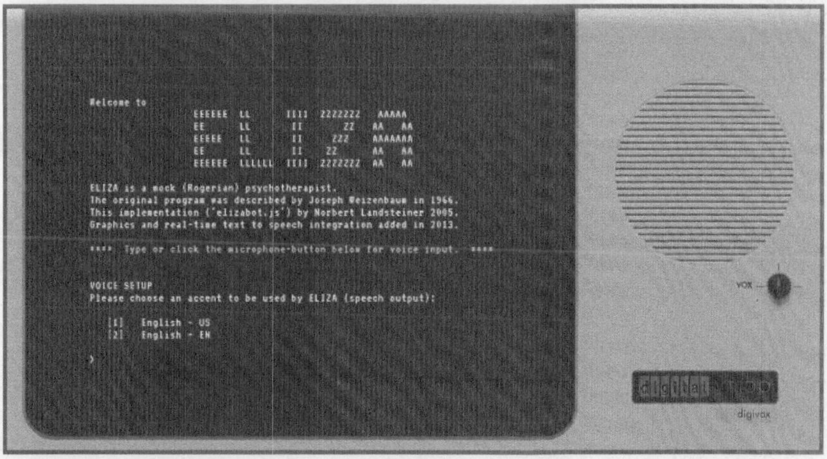

3. Choose your accent to be used by ELIZA, in this case we have type 1.

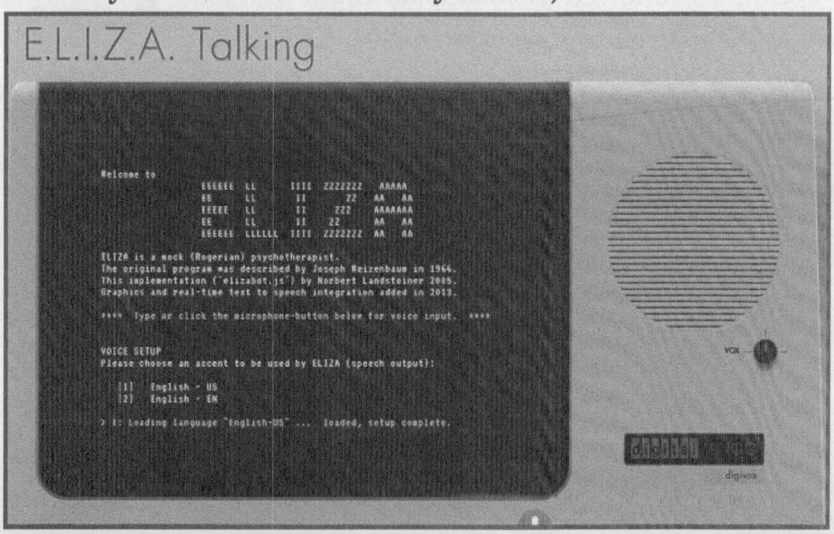

4. Loading language "English-US"....loaded, setup complete message appear.
5. Now, ELIZA will ask you for a question, "How do you do. Please tell me your problem.

6. Type whatever you want to ask, ELIZA will give you the answer (What you type will be speak by ELIZA).
7. Talk to E.L.I.ZA the very first Chabot ever created. ☺

How AI gets widespread global attention?

Artificial intelligence, initially was founded as an academic discipline in 1955, and after this for several year AI has experienced several waves of optimism, followed by disappointment and loss of funding ("AI winter"), followed by new approaches, success and renewed funding.

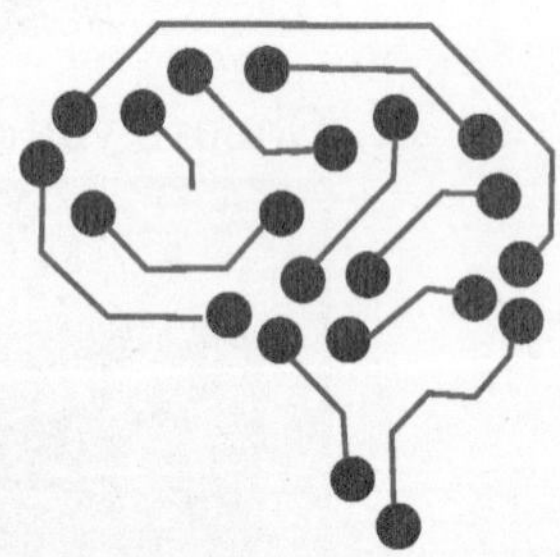

In 2015, After **AlphaGo** successfully defeated a professional **Go player**, artificial intelligence once again attracted widespread global attention.

Why AI field was founded?

AI field was founded on the assumption that human intelligence "*can be so precisely described that a machine can be made to simulate it*".

In the twenty-first century, AI techniques have become an essential part of the technology industry, helping to solve many challenging problems in computer science, software engineering, operations research, information engineering, mathematics, psychology, linguistics, philosophy, and many other fields.

What is Artificial Intelligence?

Artificial Intelligence (AI) was first coined in 1956 at Dartmouth Conference by a cognitive scientist, **John McCarthy**, at the Dartmouth Conference.

Artificial intelligence (AI) refers to the simulation of human intelligence in the machines which are programmed to think like humans and mimic the actions of humans. It can be applied to any machine which exhibits traits which are associated with a human mind such as learning and problem-solving.

DEFINITION

Artificial intelligence is based on the principle that human intelligence can be defined in a way in which a machine can easily mimic and execute the task of humans.

Extra Byte

Artificial Intelligence

- Earlier, we need to instruct the machine at every stage regarding what to do. While humans can think, and take decisions, machines cannot think and take decision on their own. In the recent years, the technological advancements have been enormous in the area of developing artificial intelligence and using it in our daily lives.

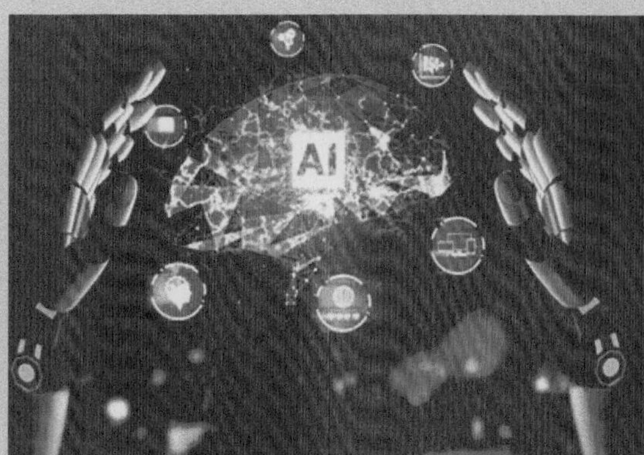

- Machine learning seamlessly become a part of our life and is now present in every field like entertainment, banking, shopping, medicine and the list goes on.
- Intelligence is the capability to obtain knowledge and skills, and then apply it to various situations without supervision.
- The branch of science and technology devoted to the creation of machines that learn and think as intelligently as human beings is known as **Artificial Intelligence (AI)**.
- John MaCarthy, father of Artificial Intelligence, define Artificial Intelligence as "*The science and engineering of making intelligent machines, especially intelligent computer programs*".
- AI is all about how the human brain thinks, learns, decides and works, when it tries to solve problems.
- Purpose of AI is to achieve improvisation in the functionality of computers in functions related to human knowledge, such as problem-solving, reasoning, and learning.
- Artificial Intelligence is made of:
  - Reasoning
  - Learning
  - Problem Solving
  - Perception
  - Linguistic Intelligence

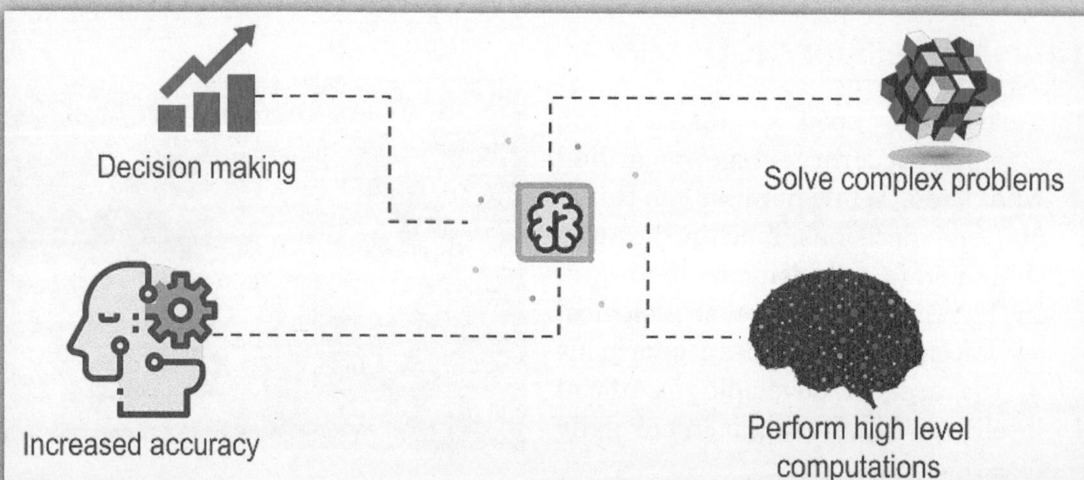

- The idea behind the introduction of AI is to create technology which allows computers and machines to function in an intelligent manner with or without human supervision.
- AI:
  - Helps to create intelligent systems which can exhibit smart behaviour with an ability to learn, validate, explain and suggest the right course of action to its users.
  - Help machines to find out solutions to complex problems and applying logic in the form of algorithms to display the required output.

- An AI system is composed of two main elements:

  a. **Agent** (human or a robot, which perceive its environment through sensors and accordingly acts on environment)

  b. **Surrounding environment**
- Common applications of AI include Natural Language Processing, Gaming, Speech Recognition, Vision Systems, Healthcare, Automotive etc.

Applications of AI

Marketing

Marketing is a way to sugar coat your products to attract more customers, and now with AI we have an algorithm or a bot for the purpose of marketing a brand or a company. We only need to search for an item on any e-commerce store, and guess what? We get all possible results related to the item.

Example: Finding the movies on Netflix.

Banking

Banks use AI-based systems to provide customer support, detect anomalies and credit card frauds.

Consider an example of HDFC Bank:

Bank has developed an AI-based Chatbot called **Electronic Virtual Assistant (EVA)**, built by Bengaluru-based Senseforth AI Research.

Eva can handle customer queries, collect knowledge from thousands of sources and provide simple answers in less than 0.4 seconds.

Finance

Machines can also learn to observe patterns in past data and predict how these patterns might repeat in the future. Financial organizations are turning to AI to improve their stock trading performance and boost profit.

Agriculture

AI can help farmers to get more from the land while using resources more sustainably. Issues such as climate change, population growth, and food security concerns have pushed the industry into seeking more innovative approaches to improve crop yield.

Automation and robotics to help farmers find more efficient ways to protect their crops from weeds.

Example: Blue River Technology has developed a robot called **See & Spray** which uses computer vision technologies like object detection to monitor and precisely spray weedicide on cotton plants.

Health Care

When it comes to saving our lives, a lot of organizations and medical care centers are relying on AI.

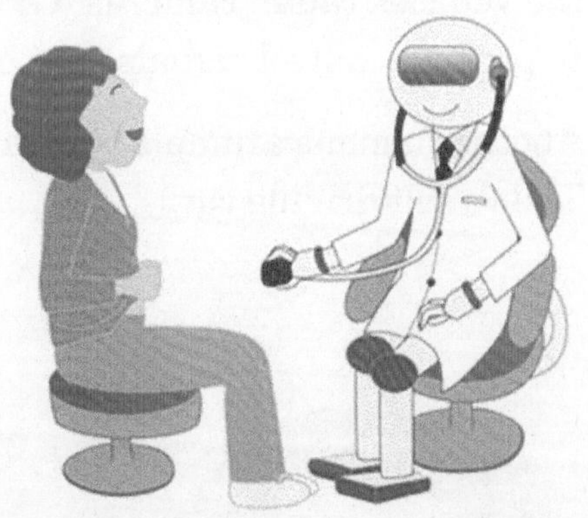

An organization called Cambio Health Care developed a clinical decision support system for stroke prevention that can give the physician a warning when there's a patient at risk of having a heart stroke.

Coala life, a company that has a digitalized device that can find cardiac diseases.

Gaming

DeepMind's AI-based AlphaGo software, which is famous for defeating Lee Sedol, the world champion in the game of GO, is one of the most significant accomplishment in the field of AI.

Other examples of Artificial Intelligence in gaming include the First Encounter Assault Recon, popularly known as F.E.A.R, which is a first-person shooter video game.

Space Exploration

Astronomers used Artificial Intelligence to sift through years of data obtained by the Kepler telescope in order to identify a distant eight-planet solar system.

Autonomous Vehicles/ Self driving cars/ Driverless cars

Self-driving cars have been a buzzword in the AI industry. The development of autonomous vehicles will revolutionaries the transport system. Companies like Waymo conducted several test drives in Phoenix before deploying their first AI-based public ride-hailing service. The AI system collects data from the vehicles radar, cameras, GPS, and cloud services to produce control signals that operate the vehicle.

Another famous example of an autonomous vehicle is Tesla's self-driving car.

Chatbots

Nowadays Virtual assistants have become a very common technology. Almost every household has a virtual assistant that controls the appliances at home. Example: Siri, Cortana.

Amazon's Echo is an example of how Artificial Intelligence can be used to translate human language into desirable actions. This device uses speech recognition and NLP to perform a wide range of tasks on your command. It can play your favourite songs, control the devices at your house, book cabs, make phone calls, order your favourite food, and check the weather conditions.

Social Media

In social media platforms like Facebook, AI is used for face verification wherein machine learning and deep learning concepts are used to detect facial features and tag your friends. Deep Learning is used to extract every minute detail from an image by using a bunch of deep neural networks.

Twitter's AI, which is being used to identify hate speech and terroristic language in tweets. It makes use of Machine Learning, Deep Learning, and Natural language processing to filter out offensive content.

Artificial Creativity

An AI-based system called MuseNet can now compose classical music that echoes the classical legends, Bach and Mozart.

Another creative product of Artificial Intelligence is a content automation tool – Wordsmith a natural language generation platform which transform your data into insightful narratives.

Tip Bot

There are Four main areas where AI has made the most possible advancements, and they are:

a. To see b. To communicate

c. To move d. To think

Activity II

Thing Translator

It takes a photo of an object and gives us a description of it using a natural language (Spanish, Italian, etc.) of our choice.

It can be easily used to learn how to pronounce things found around the house.

1. Visit the link: https://experiments.withgoogle.com/thing-translator.
2. Click on Launch Experiment

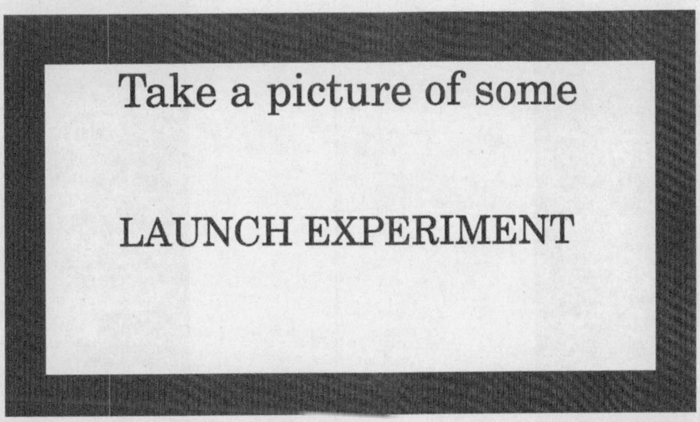

3. The following screen appear:

4. Click any picture of object around you.

5. In this case, we have clicked a picture of computer. It will give you the name of the object (we have clicked a picture of computer) in Spanish (Computadora) and English (Computer); and the following message appears:

6. You can change the language also by clicking on the word Spanish, it will then give you the list of language: FRENCH, GERMAN, ITALIAN, CHINESE, JAPANESE, KOREAN, HINDI, DUTCH.

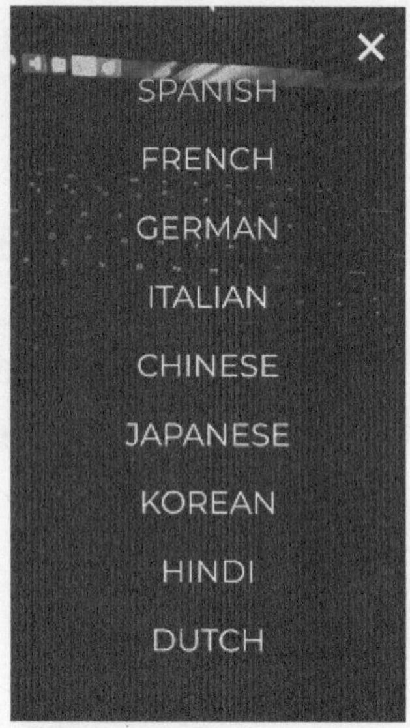

7. We choose FRENCH in this case, and now Computer in English is pronounce as Ordinateur in French.

Advantages and Disadvantages of Artificial Intelligence

Advantages	Disadvantages
Reduction in Human Error (Decisions are taken from the previously gathered information by applying a certain set of algorithms. So errors are reduced and accuracy, higher degree of precision is achieved.)	**High Costs of Creation** (Machines repairing and maintenance cost.)
Takes risks instead of Humans (AI Robot can do the risky things for us, like going to mars, defuse a bomb, and explore the deepest parts of oceans.)	**Making Humans Lazy** (AI is making humans lazy with its applications automating the majority of the work.)
Available 24x7 (AI we can make machines work 24x7 without any break.)	**Unemployment** (As AI is replacing the majority of the repetitive tasks and other works with robots, human interference is becoming less.)
Helping in Repetitive Jobs (We can productively automate tasks.)	**No Emotions** (Machines cannot develop a bond with humans which is an essential attribute when comes to Team Management.)
Digital Assistance (Chatbots to clarify the doubts and queries of the customers.)	**Lacking Out of Box Thinking** (Machines can perform only those tasks which they are designed or programmed to do.)

Memory Bot

The main goal of Artificial Intelligence is to make the machine behave intelligently by seeing, moving, thinking, and communicating.

Check your Progress - I

State whether the following statements are True or False.

a. Artificial Intelligence is the technological innovation for all new age changes happening all around us. True/False

b. Artificial intelligence, initially was founded as an academic discipline in 1965. True/False

c. AI Robot cannot do the risky things for us, like going to mars. True/False

Answer: True, False, False.

Smart Home / Home Automation

Smart homes are homes that have all the electronic devices and security systems which are controlled by the owner with the click of button. From ventilation to heating, from security to air conditioning, everything will be in your control, at a distance of a button. You click a button and you can have the entire control of which decide would be working and which would stop working, right away.

Home automation or domestics is a building automation for a home, known as **smart home or smart house**:

Definition

Smart Home is a home that can be managed remotely to control the appliances/ gadgets/systems such as TV, AC, fridge, and so on, with your device.

A home automation system will:

- Monitor and/or control the home attributes (lighting, climate, entertainment systems)
- Home security (access control and alarm systems).

When the home devices get connected with the Internet, they become the constituent of the **Internet of Things ("IoT")**.

Home automation has high potential for sharing data between family members or trusted individuals for personal security and could lead to energy saving measures with a positive environmental impact in the future.

Activity III

Shadow Art

In this, you can make shadow of pupets using your hands. The AI will then look at their hands through the camera of your mobile device and decide whether its good or not!

1. Click on the link: https://shadowart.withgoogle.com/?lang=en-us
2. The following page appears, and click on Play button:

3. Choose your date of birth, and click on next.

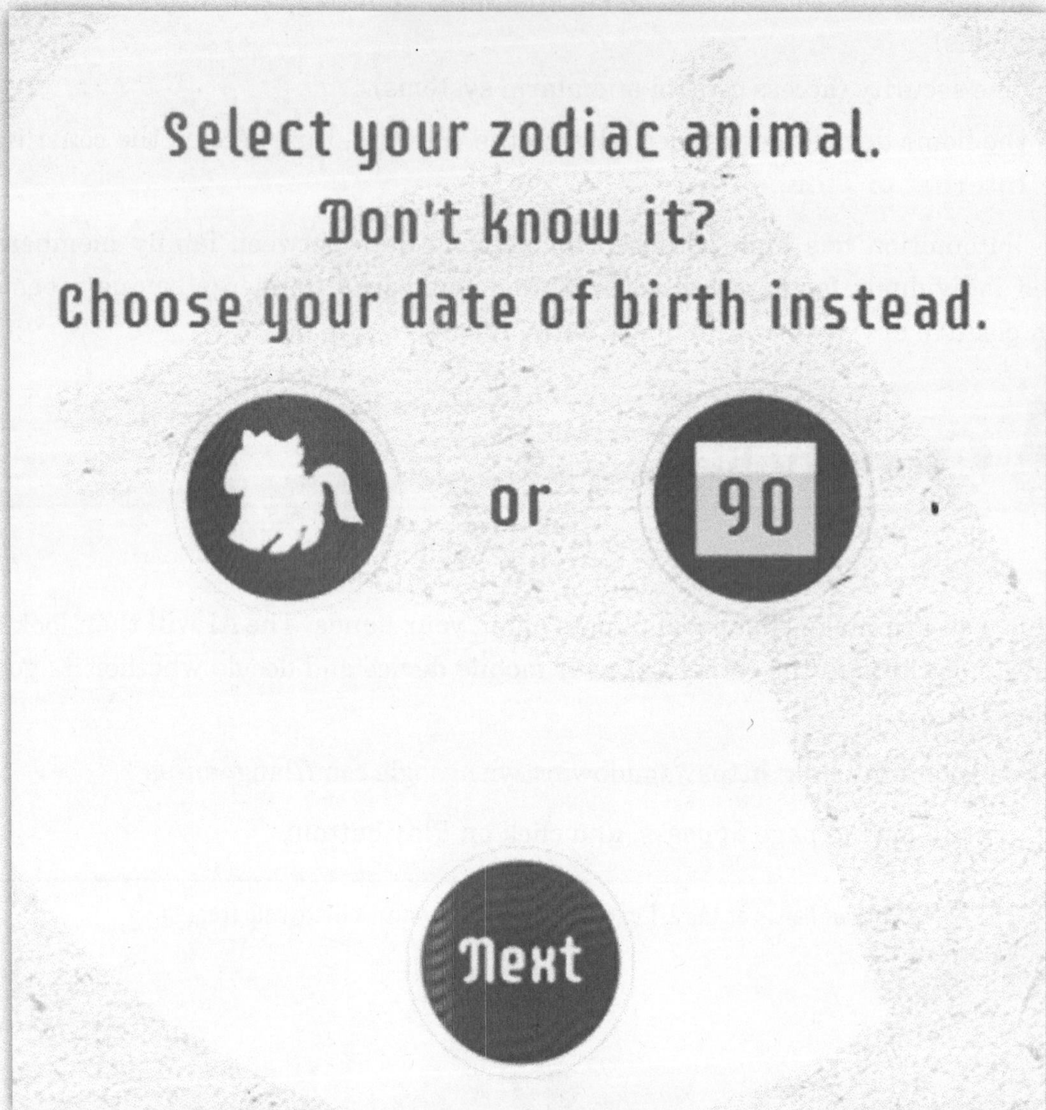

4. The following message appear, click on Begin:

5. You have to use you hand to match the outline of the horse.

Fact Bot

Most AI Bots are Female. Example: Voice assistants like Alexa, Siri a question, you will be answered by a pleasant and polite woman's voice.

Application of Smart Home/ Home Automation

- **Heating, ventilation and air conditioning (HVAC):** To have remote control of all home energy monitors over the internet.
- **Lighting control system:** A "smart" network that incorporates communication between various lighting systems.
- **Smart Grid** and a smart meter, to run washing machines.
- **Home robots and security:** Remote surveillance of security cameras over the Internet, or access control and central locking of all perimeter doors and windows.
- **Leak detection**, smoke and CO detectors
- **Indoor positioning systems (IPS)**.
- **Home automation** for the elderly and disabled.
- **Tracking the pets and babies'** movements and controlling pet access rights.
- **Air quality control**.
- **Smart Kitchen** and Connected Cooking.
- **Voice control devices** like Amazon Alexa or Google Home to control home appliances or systems.

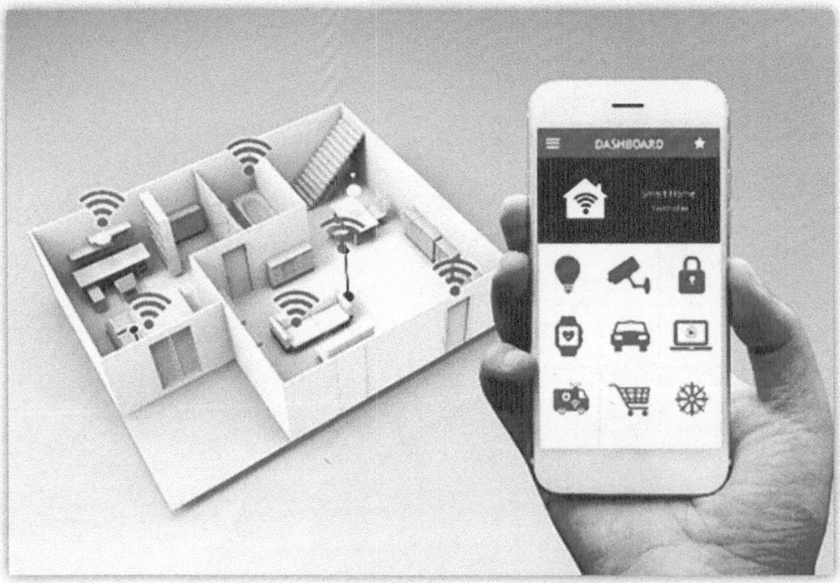

Tip Bot

A robot built in the late 1990s called **Kismet** can recognise emotions through human body language and voice tone.

Advantages and Disadvantages of Smart Home/ Home Automation

Advantages	Disadvantages
Energy Efficient (The machines, devices and appliances can all be managed and turned off immediately after usage.)	**High Cost**
Hands-free convenience	**Internet Dependency** (Without a good and strong internet connection, you will not be able to take control of your smart home.)
Enhanced Security (Easier to Lock and Unlock the Doors.)	**Need more Setup and Configuration**
Save Time with Automated Tasks	**More Technical Security Threats**

Memory Bot

Smart Homes are used for several purposes, as they can improve your comfort at home, reduce energy consumption, and enable automation of household chores.

Activity IV

List the Smart Gadgets that you want be in your Smart Home.

a. ______________________

b. ______________________

c. ______________________

d. ______________________

e. ______________________

Check your Progress - II

Fill in the Blanks.

a. Smart homes are homes that have all the ____________devices and security systems.

b. __________means the machines, devices and appliances can all be managed and turned off immediately after usage.

c. Lighting control system is a "smart" network that incorporates _________between various lighting systems.

Answer: electronic, Energy Efficient, communication

Gamification

Gamification is the process of adding game-like components to a task to encourage the participation of user participation.

Some classic game elements are:

- **Points:** It is used as visual identifiers of progress in sports, reward cards and video games.
- **Badges:** It display achievement, whether from service in the military or a gold star on school report card.
- **Leaderboards:** It is used across sports, sales teams, and in general life to present competitive placement

How is Artificial Intelligence used in Games?

Artificial Intelligence (AI) is used to generate responsive, adaptive or intelligent behaviours primarily in Non-Player Characters (NPCs) similar to human-like intelligence.

Gaming actually creates the atmosphere that inspires learners to develop skills and build an emotional connect with the subject.

DEFINITION

Gamification is set of activities and processes to solve problems by using or applying the characteristics of game elements.

Applications of Gamification

Todoist

Todoist is a productivity app that tracksuser's major work projects to simple household chores.

How it works?

The app uses gamification to prompt users to complete their tasks by rewarding them with karma points for every task they finish — and negative karma for missing a deadline.

As users collect more karma they unlock new levels, from 'Beginner' to 'Enlightened' and they can instantly share their karma score with friends on Facebook, Twitter, and Instagram.

Takeaway

Recognition is the best motivator. Social sharing creates a healthy competition with friends and co-workers that inspires users to complete their tasks.

Goibibo – Gamification for Travel

Goibibo has gamified their app to capitalize on the current trend: Indian Premier League.

How it works?

The app introduced goCashFest, where users can earn GoCash when time the Mumbai Indians play. By using the app while the team plays, users win GoCash for each 4s, 6s, 50, 100, wickets and wins during the match. This goCash is valid until the next Mumbai Indians match and can be used to make bookings on Goibibo.

Takeaway

Aim for a win-win. The popularity of IPL, in tandem with the summer holidays, has ensured that this strategy is beneficial to both Goibibo and its users. Users are spending the goCash they win on bookings for their summer holidays.

Byju's – Gamification for Education

With Byju's educational app, students master key concepts through videos, practice tests, and adaptive modules.

How it works?

Byju's uses gamification by allowing students to play games, earn reward points, and challenge each other through different quizzes and competitions. Competing with each other motivates students to work for better results.

Takeaway

Apply gamification data to improve the user experience. Tests and quizzes allow the app to measure student performance and evaluate how well they understood the concepts in each module.

Advantages and Disadvantages of Gamification

Advantages	Disadvantages
Increase Learner Engagement (Games can transform dull content into engaging and interesting experiences.)	**High Cost of Development** (Game development tends to lead to longer development time.)
Provide Instant Feedback (Educational games allow learners to progress, not by chance, but by having the right knowledge or correct response to a question or scenario.)	**Diminished Value over Time** (Games can be costly to develop, and costly to maintain.)
Boost Motivation with Features Such as Badges (Badges in gamified learning content can be as simple as virtual ribbons, stickers, or prizes that learners earn for the completion of modules or tasks within the game.)	**Games That Are Only Poorly Masked Quizzes** (Games are meant to be fun, and it's safe to say most people don't enjoy tests and quizzes.)

Fact Bot

Industries ranging from travel to banking, shopping, and entertainment rely heavily on Artificial Intelligence for using chatbots

Rock Paper Scissor game

Rock paper scissors is a hand game which is played between two people, in which each player simultaneously forms one of three shapes with an outstretched hand.

Three shapes are:

a. **Rock** (a closed fist)

b. **paper** (a flat hand)

c. **Scissors** (a fist with the index finger and middle finger extended, forming a V).

Outcomes:

- Game has only two possible outcomes: a draw, or a win for one player and a loss for the other.
- Player who decides to play rock:
  - Beat another player who has chosen scissors (as rock crushes scissors or blunts scissors)
  - Lose to one who has played paper (as paper covers rock)
  - A play of paper will lose to a play of scissors ("scissors cuts paper").
- If both players choose the same shape:
  - Game is tied and is usually immediately replayed to break the tie.

GamePlay:

- The players may count aloud to three, or speak the name of the game (e.g. "Rock! Paper! Scissors!"), either raising one hand in a fist and swinging it down with each syllable or holding it behind their back.
- Player then "throw" by extending it towards their opponent.

Activity V

To play Rock, Paper, Scissors game

1. Go to the link: https://www.afiniti.com/corporate/rock-paper-scissors
2. The following Page appears:

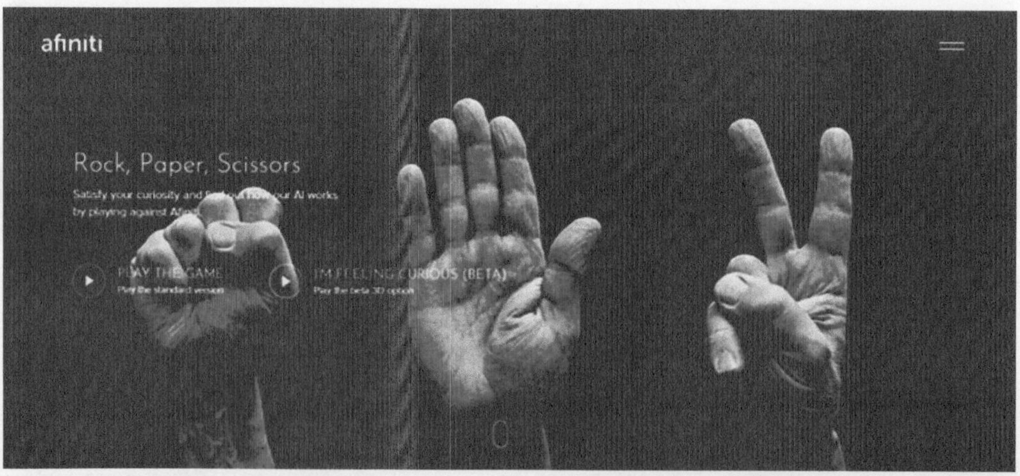

3. Click on PLAY THE GAME button.

4. Click on the shapes which you want to choose and play against the system.

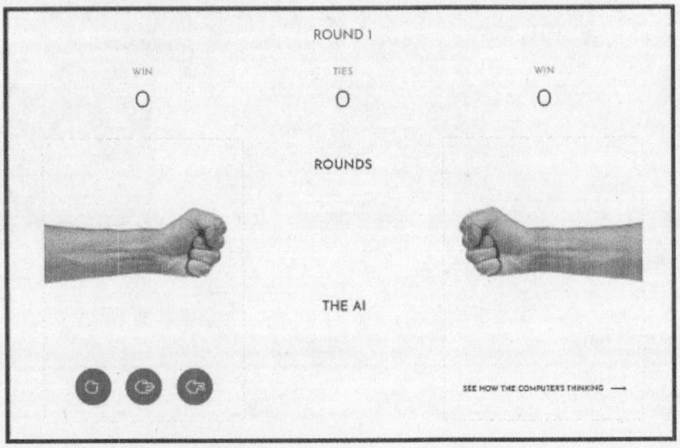

5. The result will be shown after each move.

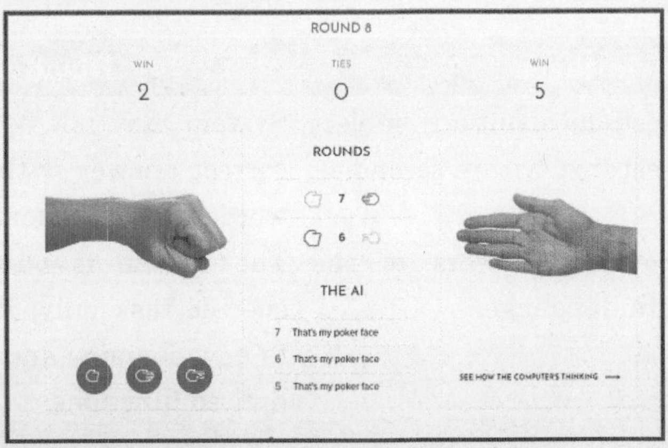

Natural Language Processing (NLP)

Natural language processing (NLP) describes the interaction among the human language and computers. It's a technology that many people use daily and has been around for years.

Examples of NLP that people use every day are:

- Spell check
- Autocomplete
- Voice text messaging
- Spam filters
- Related keywords on search engines
- Siri, Alexa, or Google Assistant

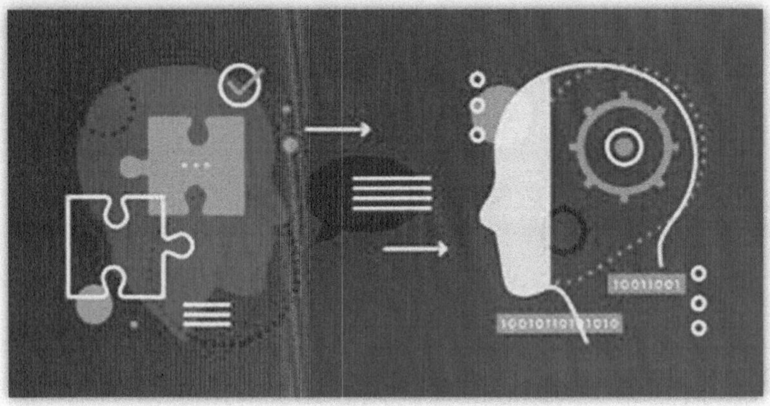

Advantages and Disadvantages of NLP

Advantages	Disadvantages
Users can ask questions about any subject and get a direct response within seconds.	System may not be able to provide the correct answer it the question is poorly worded or ambiguous.
NLP system provides answers to the questions in natural language.	The system is built for a single and specific task only; it is unable to adapt to new domains and problems because of limited functions.
NLP system offers exact answers to the questions.	NLP system doesn't have a user interface.

Tip Bot

Natural Language Processing (NLP) is about how the machines try to understand and interpret human language.

Mystery Animal

Mystery Animal is a new spin on the classic 20-questions game. The computer pretends to be an animal, and you have to guess what it is using your voice. Ask any yes-or-no question you want, like “Do you have feathers?” or “Do you sleep at night?”

Game rule:

1. A microphone must be attached to your computer.
2. The participant needs to ask a question to the computer in such a manner that will be answered by the computer in YES or NO form only.
3. The participant gets a chance of asking only 20 questions to decide upon the name of the animal.

Activity VI

To play Mystery Animal game

1. Visit the link: https://mysteryanimal.withgoogle.com/
2. The following screen appears:

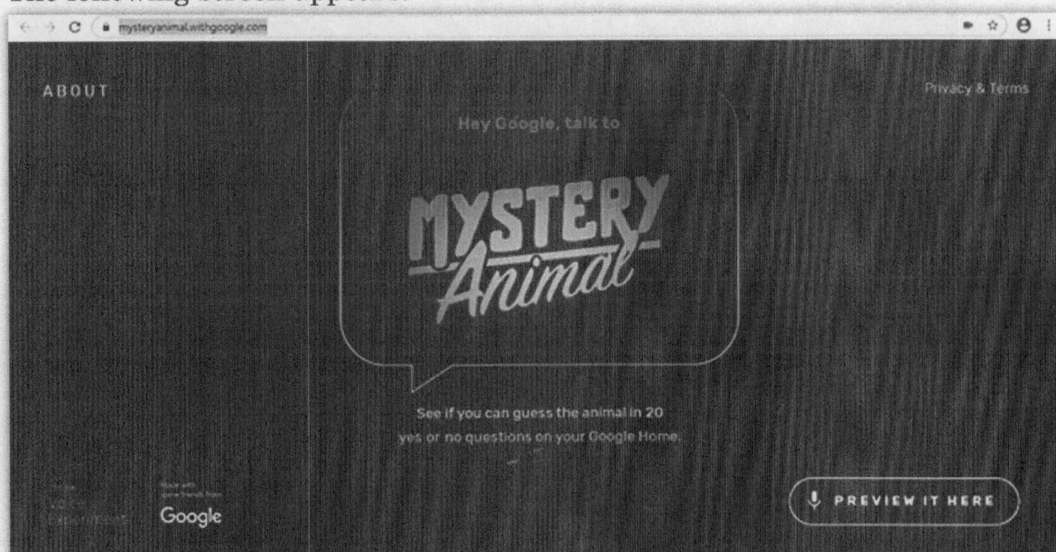

3. Click on PREVIEW IT HERE and start playing the game.

4. Click on the microphone button.

5. Start asking a question which has needs to be answered in YES or NO.
6. In this we have asked "Can you fly?" and got the answer: "No"

7. In this way, you can ask 20 questions to get the answer in Yes or No, and Identify the animal. ☺

Computer Vision

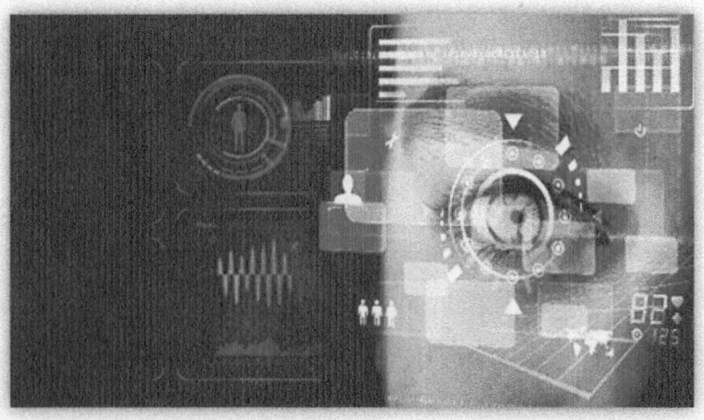

Computer vision is an interdisciplinary field that deals with how computers can be made to gain high-level understanding from digital images or videos. It seeks to automate tasks that the human visual system can do.

Computer vision is concerned with the automatic extraction, analysis and understanding of useful information from a single image or a sequence of images.

Applications of Computer Vision

- **Sports**
  - Sports Production
  - Player Tracking
- **Health and Medicine**
  - Cancer Detection
  - Cell Classification
- **Agriculture and Farming**
  - Defects in Agriculture
  - Plant Recognition
- **Transportation**
  - Autonomous Driving/self-driving cars
  - Driver Attentiveness Detection
- **Retail and Manufacturing**
  - Customer Tracking
  - Theft Detection

Advantages and Disadvantages of Computer Vision

Advantages	Disadvantages
Reliability (Computers and cameras don't have the human factor of tiredness, which is eliminated in them.)	**Necessity of specialists** (Need a professional that knows how devices of Computer Vision work.)
Accuracy (The precision of Computer Imagining and Computer Vision will ensure a better accuracy on the final product.)	**Spoiling** (Eliminate the human factor that may be good in some cases.)
A wide range of use (We can see the same computer system in several different fields and activities.)	**Failing in image processing** (When the device fails because of a virus or other software issues, it is highly probable that Computer Vision and Image Processing will fail.)

Emoji Scavenger Hunt

Emoji Scavenger Hunt is a browser-based game built with machine learning and uses your phone's camera and a neural network to try and guess what it's seeing.

Rules to play the game:

1. A webcam must be attached to your computer or the user can make use of the camera of your Smartphone / tablet.
2. The player must have access to a few of objects used in everyday lives.

Activity VII

To Play Emoji Scavenger Hunt

1. Open the link in a web browser:
   https://emojiscavengerhunt.withgoogle.com/
2. The following screen appears:

3. Click on Let's Play option.

4. Allow the camera and microphone.

5. Start playing as per the instructions coming on the screen.
6. Screen present a count of 1..2...3 and then the game starts.
7. It will give you an object to find in the room.
8. Show the image on the camera so that it can detect the image and match it with the object asked in the Find.
9. The Find box displays the icon of the image being searched to be shown in the camera.
10. If you successfully found an object then message appears as: You find an item.

Memory Bot

Computer vision is a field of study which only focused on the problem of helping computers to see.

Extra Byte

Machine Learning

- Learning that the machine learns from experience.
- Machine learning is a branch of AI which is devoted to making a machine acquire data and learn from it.
- Machine learning is the study of computer-based algorithms which is designed to automatically improve the experience through acquired learning.
- Machines are created with a built incapability to read and understand human language and make decision as accurate predictions as they can.
- So, Machine learning can be understood as a set of procedures, which deal with huge amounts of data in the to derive actionable perceptions resulting in tasks.
- In machine learning, the data and the output are run on the computer to create a program.
- Example of Machine Learning in our day-to-day life is Alexa.

Amazon Alexa/ Alexa

- It is a virtual assistant AI technology developed by Amazon.
- It was first used in the Amazon Echo smart speakers which were developed by Amazon Lab126.
- Alexa is capable of:
  - voice interaction
  - music playback
  - making to-do lists
  - controlling several smart devices using itself as a home automation system.

- How to operate Alexa:
- You can interact with Alexa in English, German, French, Italian, Spanish, Portuguese, Japanese, and Hindi.
- Users need to activate the device using a wake-word Alexa, after pressing the push button to activate Alexa's listening mode.

Check your Progress - III

Tick the correct option.

a. Artificial Intelligence (AI) is used to generate **responsive/non-responsive** behaviours primarily in Non-Player Characters (NPCs) similar to human-like intelligence.

b. Natural language processing (NLP) describes the interaction among the human language and **computers/remote control**.

c. Mystery Animal is a new spin on the classic **20/40**-questions game.

Answer: responsive, computer, 20.

TECH BOT

- **Artificial intelligence (AI):** Simulation of human intelligence in the machines which are programmed to think like humans and mimic the actions of humans.
- **Smart homes:** Homes that have all the electronic devices and security systems which are controlled by the owner with the click of button.
- **Gamification:** Adding game-like components to a task to encourage the participation of user participation.

Recap Bot

- Artificial Intelligence, or 'AI', is the technological innovation for all the new age changes which are happening all around us.
- Artificial intelligence, initially was founded as an academic discipline in 1955, and after this for several year AI has experienced several waves of optimism, followed by disappointment and loss of funding ("AI winter"), followed by new approaches, success and renewed funding.
- AI field was founded on the assumption that human intelligence "can be so precisely described that a machine can be made to simulate it".
- Artificial Intelligence (AI) was first coined in 1956 at Dartmouth Conference by a cognitive scientist, John McCarthy, at the Dartmouth Conference.
- Artificial intelligence (AI) refers to the simulation of human intelligence in the machines which are programmed to think like humans and mimic the actions of humans. It can be applied to any machine which exhibits traits which are associated with a human mind such as learning and problem-solving.
- Smart homes are homes that have all the electronic devices and security systems which are controlled by the owner with the click of button. From ventilation to heating, from security to air conditioning, everything will be in your control, at a distance of a button.
- Gamification is the process of adding game-like components to a task to encourage the participation of user participation.
- Rock paper scissors is a hand game which is played between two people, in which each player simultaneously forms one of three shapes with an outstretched hand.
- Natural language processing (NLP) describes the interaction among the human language and computers. It's a technology that many people use daily and has been around for years.
- Mystery Animal is a new spin on the classic 20-questions game. The computer pretends to be an animal, and you have to guess what it is using your voice. Ask any yes-or-no question you want, like "Do you have feathers?" or "Do you sleep at night?"
- Computer vision is an interdisciplinary field that deals with how computers can be made to gain high-level understanding from digital images or videos. It seeks to automate tasks that the human visual system can do.
- Emoji Scavenger Hunt is a browser-based game built with machine learning and uses your phone's camera and a neural network to try and guess what it's seeing.

Brain Bot

A. MULTIPLE CHOICE QUESTIONS.

1. Artificial Intelligence term was first coined in ______ by a cognitive scientist John McCarthy.

   a. 1954 ☐ b. 1955 ☐

   c. 1956 ☐ d. 1957 ☐

2. ________ is an AI software or a program which simulates a conversation with a human being.

   a. Chatbot ☐ b. Computer vision ☐

   c. NLP ☐ d. Data for AI ☐

3. AI is associated with ____ generation of computers.

   a. 2nd ☐ b. 3rd ☐

   c. 4th ☐ d. 5th ☐

4. A Smart Home is also known as:

   a. Home Automation ☐ b. Past Home ☐

   c. Non automatic Home ☐ d. Robo Home ☐

5. ________ describes the interaction among the human language and computers.

   a. Computer Vision ☐ b. Natural Language Processing ☐

   c. Data Science ☐ d. Visual system ☐

B. FILL IN THE BLANKS.

1. Artificial Intelligence, or 'AI', is the ____________innovation for all the new age changes which are happening all around us.
2. Artificial Intelligence (AI) was first coined in 1956 at Dartmouth Conference by a cognitive scientist__________, at the Dartmouth Conference.
3. _________is an interdisciplinary field that deals with how computers can be made to gain high-level understanding from digital images or videos.
4. Emoji Scavenger Hunt is a browser-based game built with ________and uses your phone's camera and a neural network to try and guess what it's seeing.

5. Gaming actually creates the atmosphere that inspires learners to develop ______ and build an emotional connect with the subject.

C. MATCH THE FOLLOWING.

Column A	Column B
1. Natural language processing	i. Emoji Scavenger Hunt
2. Computer vision	ii. Siri
3. Rock-Paper-Scissor game	iii. remote control of all home energy monitors over the internet
4. Chatbot	iv. Mystery Animal
5. Smart Home	v. Three shapes

D. ANSWER THE FOLLOWING QUESTIONS.

1. Define the term Artificial Intelligence.

____

____

2. Explain any two applications of Artificial Intelligence.

____

____

3. Explain the term Gamification.

____

____

4. Name any game where the computer predicts your next move by analysing your previous moves.

____

____

5. What do you mean by Natural Language Processing?

____

____

Lab Activity

Mitsuku, an advanced chatbots currently in existence. It won various prizes and can talk about most topics.

1. Visit the link: https://www.pandorabots.com/mitsuku/
2. The following page appears:

3. Click on Chat now; and now you can chat with Chatbot.

WORKSHEET

A. STATE WHETHER THE FOLLOWING STATEMENT ARE TRUE OR FALSE.

1. Artificial Intelligence is a branch of Computer science, which aims to create intelligent machines so that machine can think intelligently in the same manner as a human does. True/False
2. John McCarthy was a pioneer in the AI field and known as the father of Artificial intelligence. True/False
3. If a robot is able to change its own mode of work as per the external conditions, then the robot is considered intelligent. True/False
4. Computer Vision is not a domain of Artificial Intelligence. True/False
5. Machine learning is a technique which uses statistical and mathematical models. True/False

B. FILL IN THE BLANKS.

1. The main goal of Artificial Intelligence is to make the machine behave intelligently byseeing, moving, thinking, and___________.
2. There are ___________ pillars of Artificial Intelligence.
3. ___________ for AI in machine is used to predict the next move of human from previous movescollected by the machine.
4. Natural Language Processing is a technology with which the machine is able tounderstand human language and perform an action based on the ___________.
5. Computer Vision is a technology with which the machine can see around and also collect ___________ from images.

C. ANSWER THE FOLLOWING QUESTIONS.

1. What does Computer Vision mean?

   ____

   ____

2. What is the main goal of AI?

   ____

   ____

3. Name the three pillars of AI.

4. Write any one advantage and disadvantage of AI.

5. Explain the use of Smart Home.

Notes

Quiz Card

TICK THE CORRECT ANSWER.

1. What is Artificial intelligence?
   a. Gifting intelligence to Computer
   b. Program your own intelligence
   c. To make a Machine intelligent
   d. Playing a game on computer
2. A.M. turing developed a technique which is used for determining whether a computer could or could not demonstrate the artificial Intelligence, and this technique is known as __________
   a. Turing Test
   b. Data Science
   c. Boolean Algebra
   d. Computer Vision
3. __________ is a component of an expert system.
   a. knowledge base
   b. computer
   c. human
   d. animal
4. __________ is a computer vision technique which relies on image templates.
   a. Monocular vision
   b. binocular vision
   c. model-based vision
   d. robot vision
5. ______University/School was not among the early leaders in Artificial Intelligence research.
   a. Dartmouth University
   b. Stanford University
   c. Massachusetts Institute of Technology
   d. Harvard University
6. _________is the "father" of artificial intelligence.
   a. Alan Turning
   b. John McCarthy
   c. Allen Newell
   d. David Levy
7. What are the main goals of AI?
   a. To Create Expert Systems
   b. To extract Human Intelligence
   c. To create dump machine
   d. To create machine
8. __________ areas can contribute to build an intelligent system.
   a. Philosophy
   b. Biology
   c. Sociology
   d. All of the above
9. Which of the following is an application of AI?
   a. Gaming
   b. Non Expert Systems
   c. Visual Systems
   d. Non-gaming system
10. ___________is used to adjust the house temperature
    a. Smart Home device
    b. Smartphone
    c. Smart Car
    d. Remote control

2 AI APPLICATIONS

Structure Bot

In this chapter, we will discuss:

- Artificial Intelligence (AI) in various fields
- Skills required for AI ready future job
- AI applications using the Research template
- Ethical concerns of AI

Objective Bot

At the end of this chapter, you should be able to:

- Know how AI has been affecting jobs in various industries
- Learn the theme-based research of various local case studies
- Understand the home communication and collaborative skills to design activities

Introduction

Artificial Intelligence in daily life is used for:

- Checking your schedules of daily task
- Looking for directions (Google Map)
- Music and movie recommendations by digital assistants (Netflix)
- Chatbots (Alexa, Siri)
- Self driving car
- Parking assistance
- Automatic E-mail replies
- Search on a web browser
- Online purchases
- Travel bookings

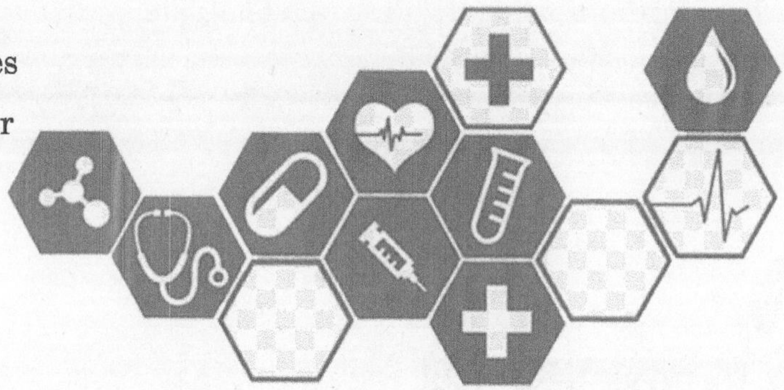

Fact Bot

Stephen Hawking's take said that #AI, wither will be "the best, or the worst thing, ever to happen to humanity. We do not yet know which."

Areas where AI is used

Music and Media

Artificial Intelligence is helping users to find music and media of their choice on apps like Spotify, Netflix, or YouTube.

Smart Home Devices

Artificial Intelligence is used in smart home devices to adjust the house temperature and lighting based on the preferences.

Smart phones

AI integration in mobile technology is bringing features like face detection, virtualreality elements, photo editor.

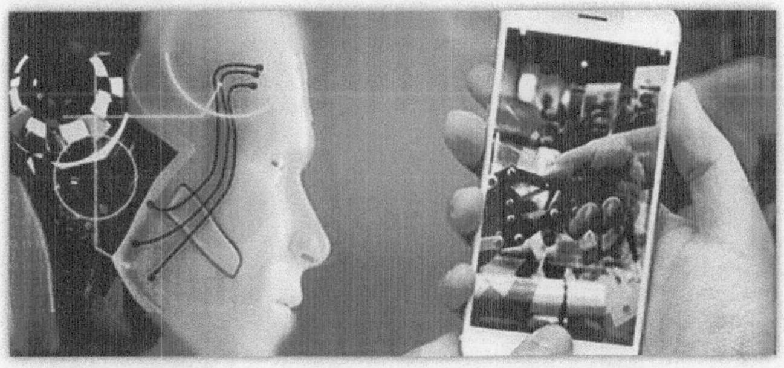

Social Media Feeds

Feeds that you see in your timeline along with the notifications that you receive from these apps is curated mainly by AI.

Video Games

Game such as PUBG or Fortnite essentially starts playing against a couple of AI-powered bots and then move to play against real players in consecutive levels.

Navigation and Travel

Suggest real-time traffic data (Google Maps).

Security and Surveillance

Object recognition and facial recognition are monitored by AI.

Activity I

Sketch-RNN (Draw Single Image)

To draw image with a recurrent neural network model. Once you start drawing the object, Sketch-RNN will provide many possible ways to continue drawing form where you left off.

1. **Go to the link:** https://experiments.withgoogle.com/sketch-rnn-demo
2. Click on Launch Experiment.

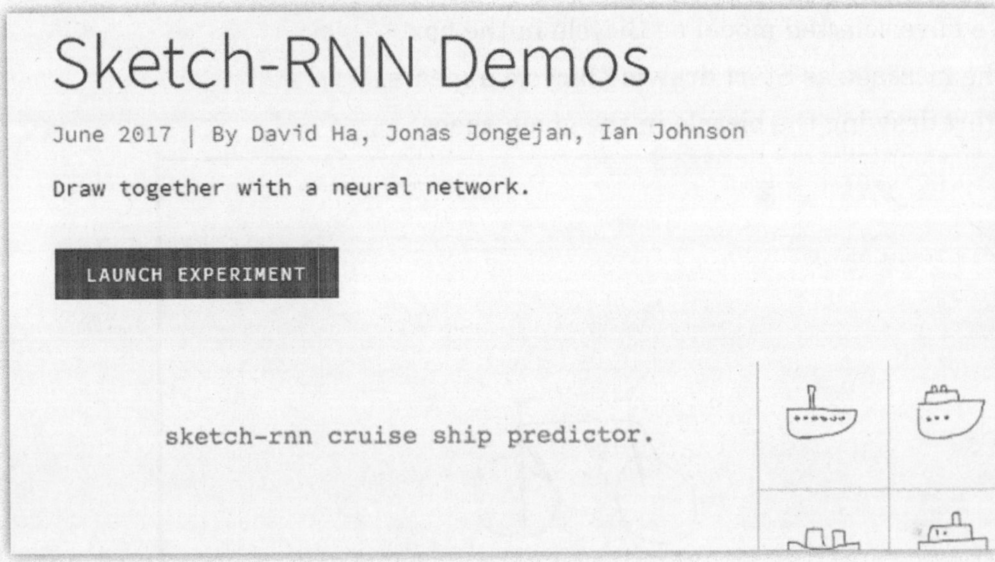

3. Click on the try the Sketch-RNN demo.

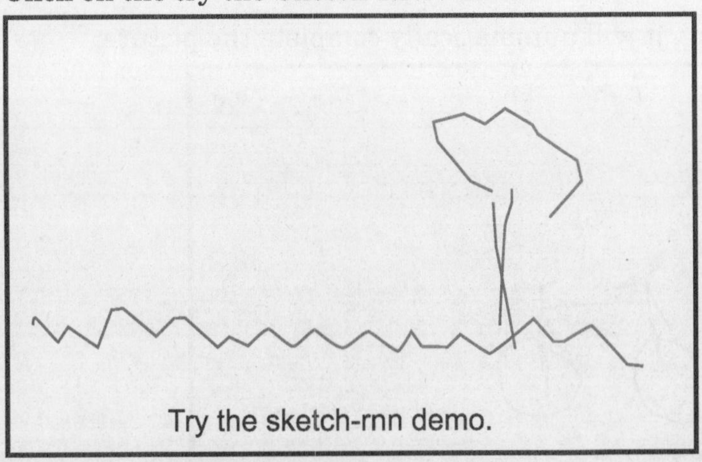

4. You can see the following screen:

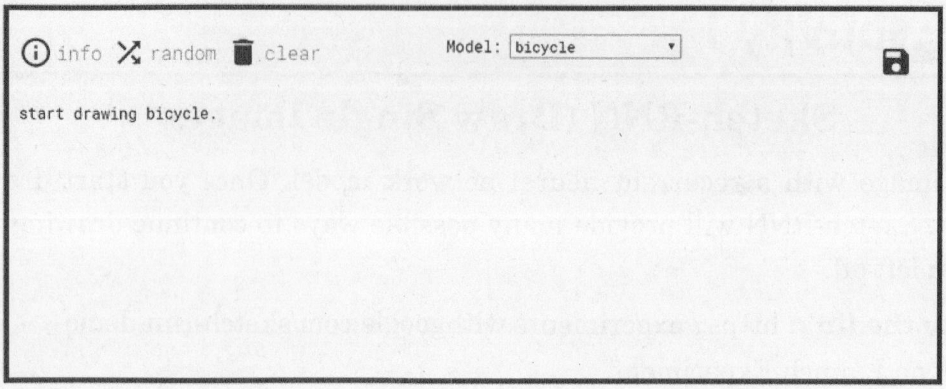

5. We have selected model as Bicycle in the box.
6. The message as Start drawing bicycle appears.
7. Start drawing the bicycle in the given space.

8. Where you stop drawing, it will automatically complete the picture:

DEFINITION

Artificial Intelligence has various applications and is becoming essential for today's time because it can solve complex problems with an efficient way in multiple industries, such as Healthcare, entertainment, finance, education, and so on.

Activity II

Identify and write the areas where Artificial Intelligence plays a major role.

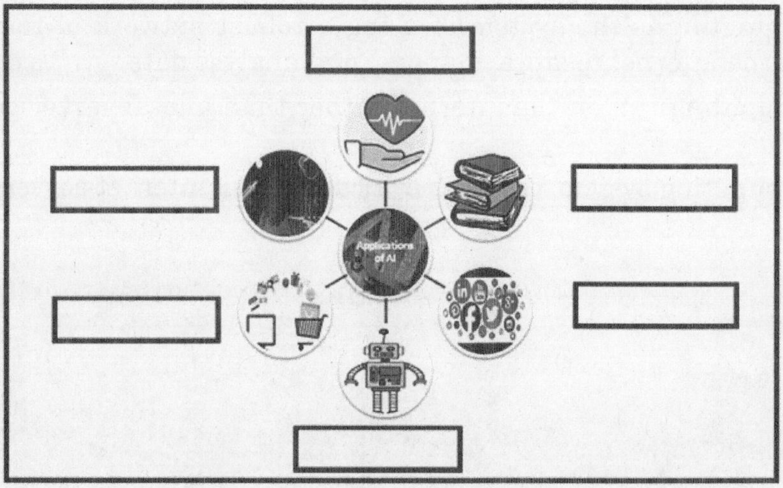

Hint: Healthcare, Education, Space exploration, E-commerce, Robotics, Social media

Check your Progress - I

State whether the following statements are True or False.

a. Artificial Intelligence is helping users to find music and media of their choice on apps like Spotify, Netflix, or YouTube. True/False

b. Artificial Intelligence is not used in smart home devices to adjust the house temperature and lighting based on the preferences. True/False

c. AI integration in mobile technology is bringing features like face detection, virtual reality elements, and photo editor. True/False

Answer: True, False, True.

Extra Byte

EXPOSURE TO AI USING APPS

- Application Programming Interface or API is a set of commands, protocols and functions that are used in programming to create software which is capable of interacting with an external system.
- APIs are designed to work with the cloud services as most of the data used tends to be stored on the cloud.

Cloud Computing

- Cloud Computing is the system of using a robust network of remote servers hosted on the internet to store, manage, and analyse data.
- Cloud Computing run on the internet rather than a local server or a personal computer.
- A cloud computing system keeps its critical data on internet servers.

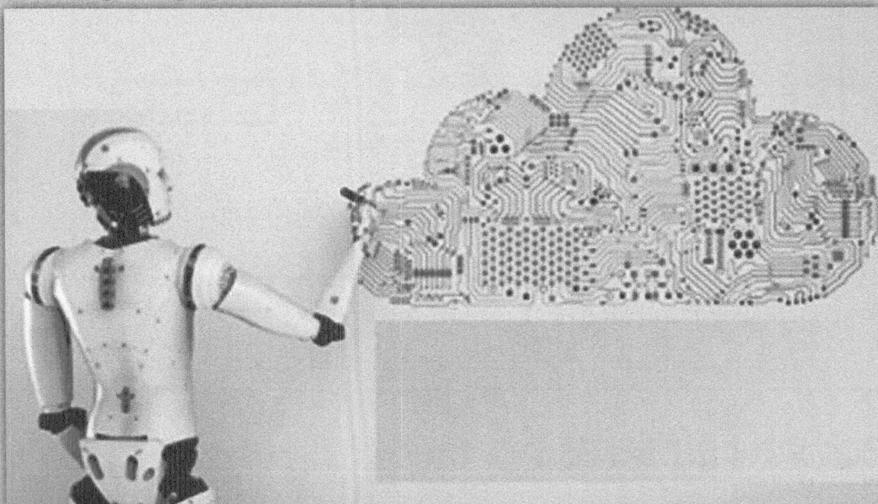

Face & Emotion Recognition

The face recognition application is built to detect one or more than one human face and get back face rectangles in addition to the various attributes of the face.

The API is designed to detect faces in the images and identify them.

Few face attributes feature which are available are:

- Age
- Emotion
- Gender
- Pose
- Smile and
- Facial hair

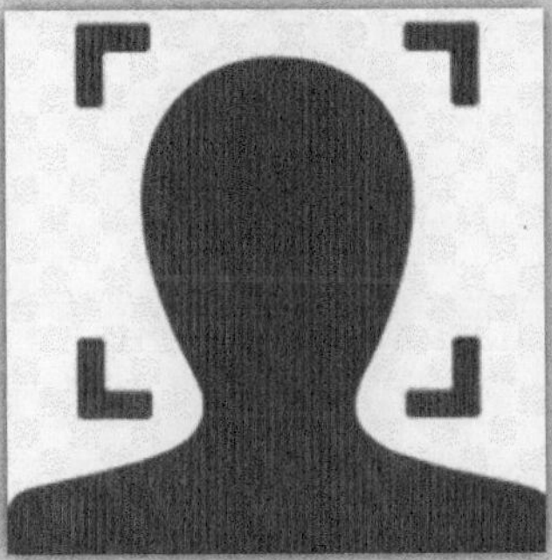

Face identification

The face API permits searching, identifying and matching faces saved in a repository of up to 1 million people.

Face Search

The API is designed to analyse and find faces that tend to look similar.

Face Grouping

The API is designed to organize images of unidentified people based on the presence of a common face.

Emotion Recognition

The Face API can be used for recognising the emotion of a human face. The API can distinguish emotions such as anger, happiness, contempt, fear, disgust, sadness, and even surprise.

Speech Authentication

Capable of listening to a live voice of a recording and then converting the same to text. It is very powerful verification tool where the unique voice modulations of a person can be used to ascertain the identity of the person and validate the same.

Conversation Transcription

It capture the speech in the real time scenario and aid in transcription. This enables participants to engage in the discussion completely.

Speech Transcription

It converts spoken audio to text. It calls the API to recognize audio coming from the microphone, from other real-time streaming audio sources or from a recorded audio file. As the audio is directed to the server, limited recognition results are reverted once the request for the file is placed.

Text Analytics

Text analytics is the process of converting unstructured text data into meaningful data for analysis, to measure feedback, sentimental analysis and other studies. Text analysis uses many linguistic, statistical, and machine learning techniques.

Video Indexer

A Video Indexer gives you access to additional video insights, like the number of earned actions that you've generated or how long potential customers view your video ad for. It is recommended especially if you have linked your YouTube channel to your browser Ads account.

Personal Vs. Digital Assistant

Personal Assistant	Digital Assistant
A personal assistant is a person working exclusively for one particular person.	A digital assistant is a computer program designed to assist people.
Example: Peon, Secretary, Assistant	**Example:** Cortana, Alexa, Siri

Cortana

Cortana is Microsoft's digital assistant which helps you to get things done. You have to signed into your Microsoft account to do.

Once you signed it, click the blue text "Learn how I say, 'Hey Cortana.'" The search program will guide you through a series of tests to make sure your microphone is working correctly, and then it will "learn" your voice so that you can instantly activate the Cortana window with the phrase from any screen.

Cortana helps you to:

- Set reminders
- Identify a song
- Search the Web with a browser
- Perform Calculations and Conversions
- Find Facts
- Check the Weather
- Get Directions
- Set Alarms
- Launch Programs
- Send Email

Research Template

Research is a process of systematic inquiry that entails:

- collection of data
- documentation of critical information
- analysis and interpretation of that data/information

in accordance with suitable methodologies set by specific professional fields and academic disciplines.

Research is conducted to evaluate the validity of a hypothesis or an interpretive framework; to assemble a body of substantive knowledge and findings for sharing them in appropriate manners; and to generate questions for further inquiries.

Step-by-step approach to starting and completing a research paper:

a. **Choosing a topic: Interest, information, and focus**

   Your job will be more pleasant, and you will be more apt to retain information if you choose a topic that holds your interest.

b. **Preliminary reading & record keeping**

   Gather some index cards or a small notebook and keep them with you as you read.

c. **Organizing: Mind map or outline**

   Based on your preliminary reading, draw up a working mind map or outline. Include any important, interesting, or provocative points, including your own ideas about the topic.

d. **Formulating a thesis: Focus and craftsmanship**

   Write a well defined, focused, three- to five-point thesis statement, but be prepared to revise it later if necessary.

e. **Researching: Facts and examples**

   Try the internet, electronic databases, reference books, newspaper articles, and books for a balance of sources. For each source, write down on an index card, the publication information you will need for your works cited (MLA) or bibliography (APA) page.

f. **Rethinking: Matching mind map and thesis**

   After you have read deeply and gathered plenty of information, expand or revise your working mind map or outline by adding information, explanations, and examples.

g. **Drafting: Beginning in the middle**

Write the body of the paper, starting with the thesis statement and omitting for now the introduction.

h. **Revising: Organization and attribution**

Read, revise, and make sure that your ideas are clearly organized and that they support your thesis statement.

i. **Writing: Intro, conclusion, and citations**

Write the final draft. Add a one-paragraph introduction and a one-paragraph conclusion.

j. **Proofreading: Time and objectivity**

On your final read, check for grammar, punctuation, correct word choice, adequate and smooth transitions, sentence structure, and sentence variety.

Tip Bot

Deep Blue was the first AI robot, which was made in 1996. It was a chess-playing computer which won its first game against a World Champion on 10 February 1996.

Activity III

Let us explore the theme "Space Exploration in AI" in detail and see how AI is influencing it with its new technological advancements.

1. **Click on the link and read the article:**
https://read.hyperight.com/how-nasa-uses-ai-and-machine-learning-for-spaceexploration/#:~:text=AI%20has%20proven%20its%20great,navigation%2C%20monitoring%20and%20system%20control.
2. **Make entries in the Research Template as given:**

Research Theme: Space Exploration

- Artificial intelligence and machine learning made a transformative impact on innumerable fields and industries.
- It led the way in automating and optimising processes, and creating new business opportunities.
- Now, these advanced technologies are implemented in research and development out of our atmosphere and into space.
- NASA uses AI and Machine Learning for space exploration.

- AI has proven its great potential and a game-changer in space exploration.
- In Space exploration, AI is used for Charting unmarked galaxies, stars, black holes, and studying cosmic events, communication, autonomous starcraft navigation, monitoring and system control.

AI-powered space journey: How NASA Uses AI and Machine Learning for space exploration

- NASA is continuously making progress in AI applications for space exploration to automate image analysis for galaxy/planet/star classification.
- Developing an autonomous spacecraft that could avoid space debris without human intervention, create communication networks more efficient and distortion-free by using an AI-based cognitive radio.

How NASA uses AI and Machine Learning for space exploration

- Most important applications of AI for NASA is the development of robot who will roam the surface of other planets.
- Robots are required to make decisions and avoid obstacles on the rough surface while determining the best route without specific commands from the mission control.

Research Scientist who are working on the project:

- **Shreyansh Daftry:** Research Scientist at NASA Jet Propulsion Laboratory (JPL) in Pasadena, California, who is working at the intersection of Artificial Intelligence and Space Technology to develop the next generation of robots for Earth, Mars and beyond.

Skills

- Among the most essential skills workers need for any space exploration project is the ability to work well as part of a team.
- Interpersonal skills are crucial for sharing discoveries and ideas—including those from people other than colleagues.
- Workers in space exploration also should be curious, adaptable, and diligent. And they must be able to work well under pressure.

Challenges

- As satisfying as a career in space exploration may be, some of these jobs are stressful. Pushing the limits of science and technology often comes with high stakes.
- Workers also say that keeping up with technology is a constant challenge.

Launching a space career

Some skills are common across all careers in space exploration. But you might need education, experience, or training specific to the occupation you want to enter.

Education, experience, and on-the-job training that is typically required to enter some of these occupations are:

Occupation	Education	Work experience in a related occupation	On-the-job training
Scientists			
Astronomers	Doctoral or professional degree	None	None
Atmospheric and space scientists	Bachelor's degree	None	None
Physicists	Doctoral or professional degree	None	None
Engineers			
Aerospace engineers	Bachelor's degree	None	None
Computer hardware engineers	Bachelor's degree	None	None
Electronics engineers	Bachelor's degree	None	None
Mechanical engineers	Bachelor's degree	None	None
Technicians			
Aerospace engineering and operations technicians	Associate's degree	None	None
Avionics technicians	Associate's degree	None	None
Life, physical, and social science technicians, all other	Associate's degree	None	None

Activity IV

To draw image with a recurrent neural network model.

Once you start drawing the object, Sketch-RNN will provide many possible ways to continue drawing form where you left off.

1. **Go to the link:** https://experiments.withgoogle.com/sketch-rnn-demo
2. Click on Launch Experiment.

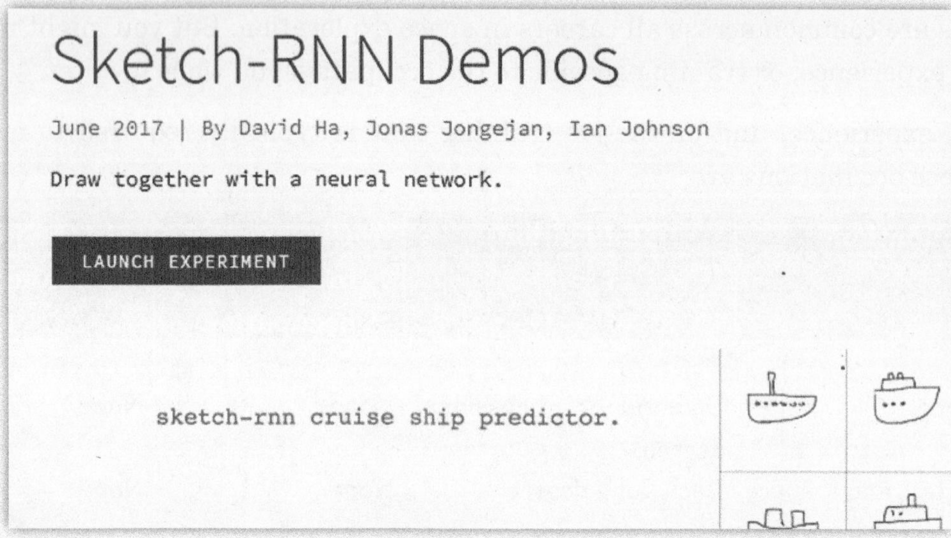

3. Click on the Multiple Predict Demo.

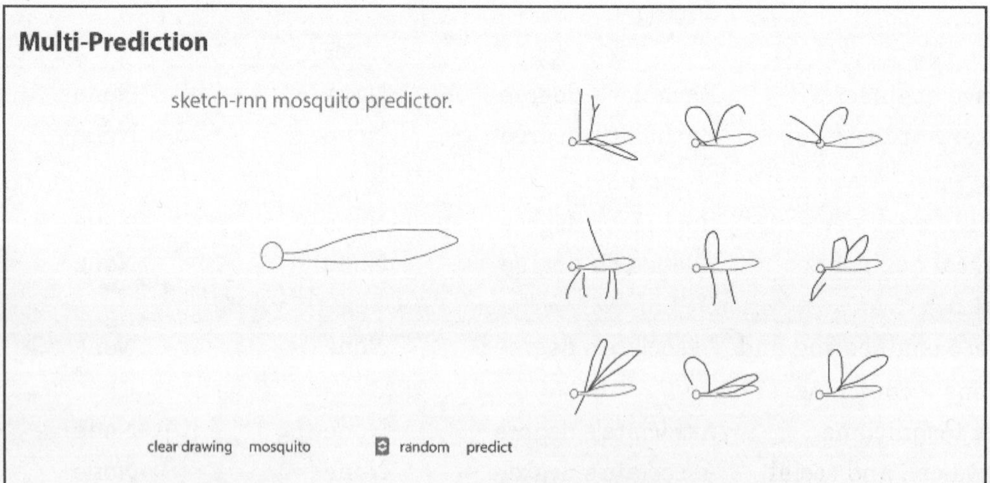

Multiple Predict Demo

4. Start drawing the bicycle in the given space.

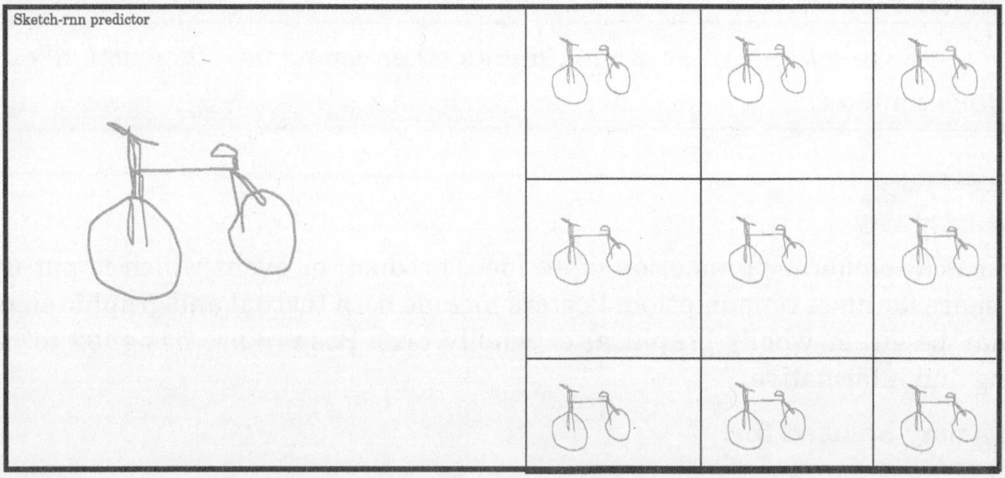

6. Where you stop drawing, it will automatically complete the picture:

Check your Progress - II

Fill in the Blanks.

a. Research is a process of systematic inquiry that entails collection of________.

b. ________ is conducted to evaluate the validity of a hypothesis or an interpretive framework.

c. Read, revise, and make sure that your ideas are clearly _______and support your thesis statement.

Answer: data, Research, organized.

Memory Bot

Google has a Quantum AI Lab where, unlike other companies, they actually own a quantum computer.

Poster

A poster is a temporary promotion of an idea, product, or event which is put up in a public space for mass consumption. Posters include both textual and graphic elements, or it may be either wholly graphical or wholly text. Posters are designed to be eye-catching and informative.

Posters may be used for:

- Advertisement of events, musicians, and films
- propagandists
- protestors
- reproductions of artwork

Focus of making poster is to make stress on the main idea and has to be presented in such a manner that it talks about the topic clearly by itself.

Key elements which poster must contain:

- Title of the advertisement (Job designation)
- Short description about the company
- Number of vacancies and the post should be clearly mentioned
- Age and gender for the suitable post
- Location
- Remuneration
- Qualification
- Mode of communication
- Contact details

Definition

A poster is a temporary promotion of an idea, product, or event which is put up in a public space for mass consumption. Posters include both textual and graphic elements, or it may be either wholly graphical or wholly text. Posters are designed to be eye-catching and informative.

Activity V

Strange poster generator

A poster generator that uses AI image recognition to transform whatever image you upload into a Stranger Things poster.

1. Go to the link: http://evenstranger.pw/
2. The following Screen appears, and click on Upload an Image.

3. We have upload beverage can image:

4. It will take few seconds to create an image. The following output screen appears:

In the same way, you can draw other strange images, by clicking n Go again. ☺

Fact Bot

With AI, ability to nap in your car while you commute to work is much closer than you think.

Activity VI

Design one advertisement for the requirement of Aerospace engineers for XYZ Space Company.

Information you need to make a poster:

- Title of the Advertisement
- Short description about the company
- Number of vacancies and the post
- Gender for the suitable post

- Location (State in which it is required)
- Salary in INR
- Educational Qualification and experience (if any) needed for the post
- Mode of applying (E-mail, postal)
- E-mail:
- Contact address and phone number for correspondence

Required Aerospace engineers

XYZ Space Company has announced vacancy for Aerospace engineer for space exploration to automate image analysis for galaxy/planet/star classification.

Total Posts	1
Gender	Female
Location	Delhi
Salary	1,50,000 INR
Educational Qualification	Bachelors degree in Aeronautical Engineering
Experience	2 years
E-mail your resume at	Hr@ xyzspace.com
Contact	XYZ Space Company 10, ABC road Pin: 123456

Job Advertisement Poster:

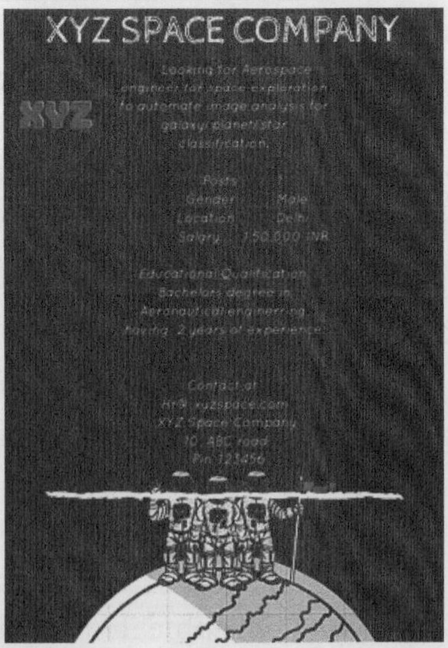

Tip Bot

Artificial intelligence has deeply rooted itself into every sphere and it's highly unlikely that it will ever disappear from our lives.

Check your Progress - III

Tick the correct option.

a. A poster is a **temporary/permanent** promotion of an idea, product, or event.

b. Posters include **both/any** one of either textual or graphic elements.

c. Posters **are/are not** designed to be eye-catching and informative.

Answer: temporary, both, are

TECH BOT

- **Video Games:** Game such as PUBG or Fortnite essentially starts playing against a couple of AI-powered bots and then move to play against real players in consecutive levels.
- **Navigation and Travel:** Suggest real-time traffic data (Google Maps).
- **Security and Surveillance:** Object recognition and facial recognition are monitored by AI.

Recap Bot

- Artificial Intelligence in daily life is used for Checking your schedules of daily task, Looking for directions (Google Map), Music and movie recommendations by digital assistants (Netflix)
- Research is a process of systematic inquiry that entails:
  - o collection of data
  - o documentation of critical information
  - o analysis and interpretation of that data/information in accordance with suitable methodologies set by specific professional fields and academic disciplines.
- A poster is a temporary promotion of an idea, product, or event which is put up in a public space for mass consumption. Posters include both textual and graphic elements, or it may be either wholly graphical or wholly text. Posters are designed to be eye-catching and informative.

Brain Bot

A. MULTIPLE CHOICE QUESTIONS.

1. Artificial Intelligence in daily life is used for:
   a. Checking your schedules of daily task ☐
   b. Looking for directions (Google Map) ☐
   c. Music and movie recommendations by digital assistants (Netflix) ☐
   d. All of the above ☐
2. Research is a process of systematic inquiry that entails:
   a. collection of data ☐
   b. documentation of critical information ☐
   c. analysis and interpretation of that data/information ☐
   d. All of the above ☐
3. Your job will be more pleasant, and you will be more apt to retain information if you choose a topic that holds your:
   a. Interest ☐ b. Information ☐
   c. Focus ☐ d. Topic ☐
4. Preliminary reading & record keeping means:
   a. Based on your preliminary reading, draw up a working mind map or outline. ☐
   b. Write a well defined, focused, three- to five-point thesis statement. ☐
   c. Try the internet, electronic databases, reference books, newspaper articles, and books for a balance of sources. ☐
   d. Gather some index cards or a small notebook and keep them with you as you read. ☐
5. A poster is a temporary promotion of an:
   a. Idea ☐ b. Product ☐
   c. Event ☐ d. All of the above ☐

B. FILL IN THE BLANKS.

1. Research is a process of systematic inquiry that entails ________of data
2. Research is conducted to the ________of a hypothesis or an interpretive framework.
3. Your job will be more pleasant, and you will be more apt to retain information if you choose a _________ that holds your interest.
4. Preliminary reading & record keeping means gather some _____or a small notebook and keep them with you as you read.
5. Based on your preliminary reading, draw up a working ________ or outline.

C. MATCH THE FOLLOWING.

	Column A		Column B
1.	Music and media AI integration	i.	
2.	Smart Home Devices AI integration	ii.	
3.	Smart phones AI integration	iii.	
4.	Social Media Feeds AI integration	iv.	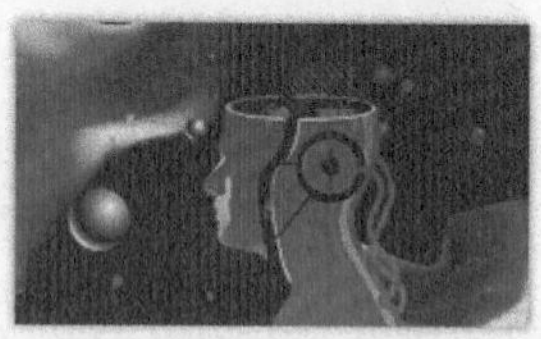
5.	Navigation and Travel AI integration	v.	

D. ANSWER THE FOLLOWING QUESTIONS.

1. Define the use of AI in security and surveillance.

2. Explain any two applications areas of AI.

3. Explain the term Research template.

4. Write the use of AI on video and games.

5. What do you mean by poster?

Lab Activity

Sketch-RNN (Variational Autoencoder Demo)

To draw image with a recurrent neural network model. Once you start drawing the object, Sketch-RNN will provide many possible ways to continue drawing form where you left off.

1. Go to the link: https://experiments.withgoogle.com/sketch-rnn-demo
2. Click on Launch Experiment.

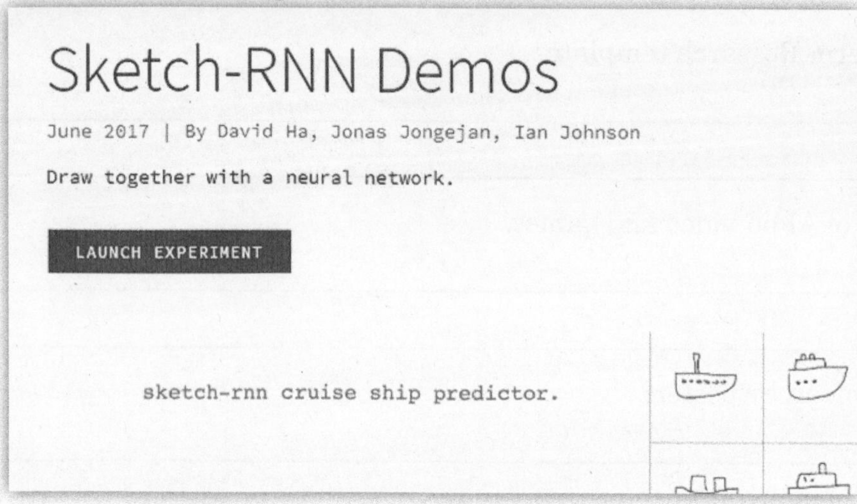

3. Click on the Variational Autoencoder Demo.

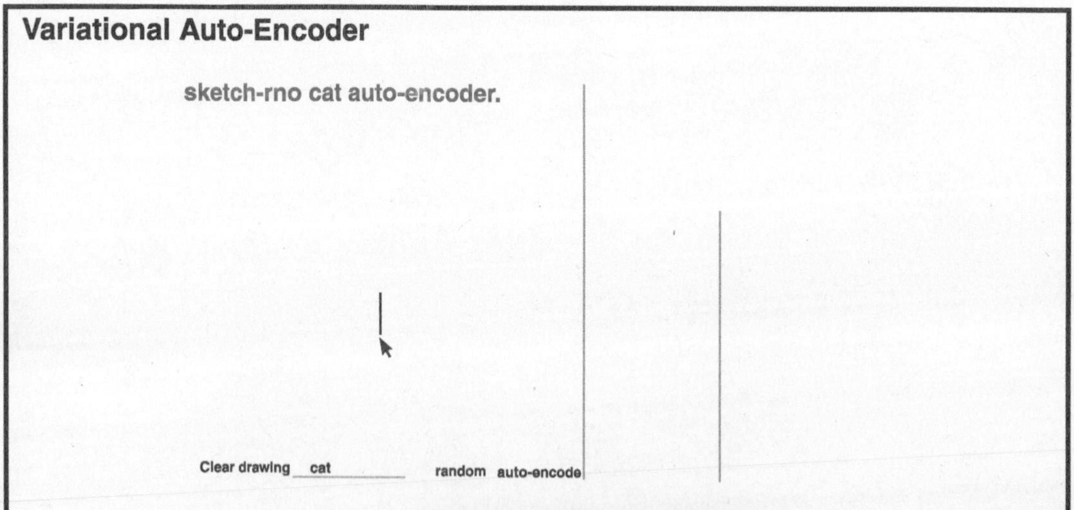

Variational Autoencoder Demo

4. You can see the following screen:

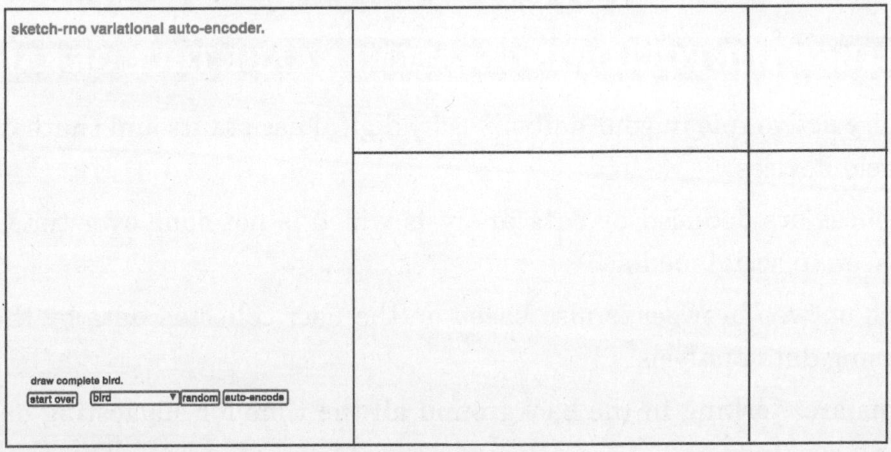

5. Start drawing the bird in the given space.

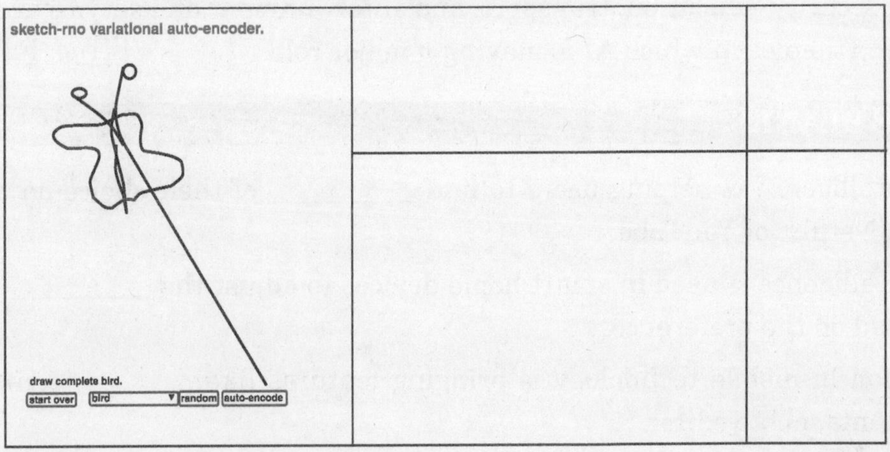

6. Where you stop drawing, it will automatically complete the picture:

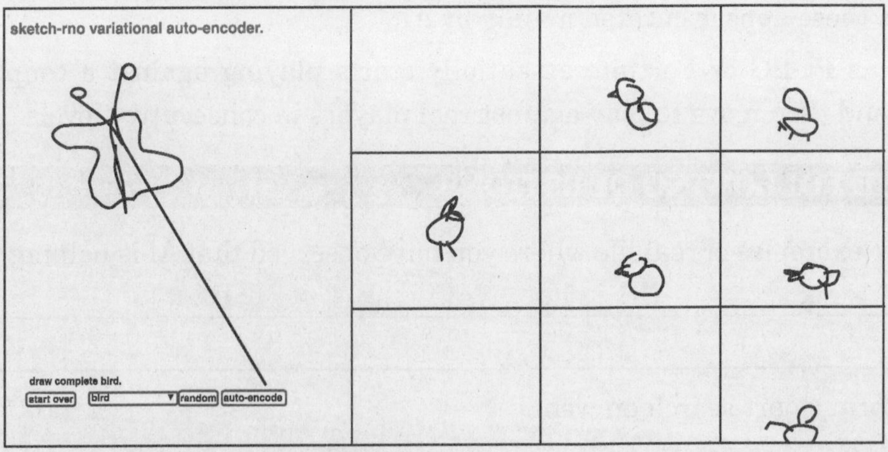

WORKSHEET

A. STATE WHETHER THE FOLLOWING STATEMENT ARE TRUE OR FALSE.

1. AI plays a very active role in your daily lives by digital assistants and chatbots on your hand-held devices. True/False
2. User preferences are deduced by data analysis which is not done over time and that can be seen in social media. True/False
3. Smart search on web browser is also based on the user collected data by the AI assistance using data analysis. True/False
4. AI algorithms are working in the background all the time for suggesting online purchases and bookings. True/False
5. Healthcare, security, education, transport, and entertainment and service are the main domains/themes in which AI is playing a major role. True/False

B. FILL IN THE BLANKS.

1. Artificial Intelligence is helping users to find __________ of their choice on apps like Spotify, Netflix, or YouTube.
2. Artificial Intelligence is used in smart home devices to adjust the __________ and lighting based on the preferences.
3. AI integration in mobile technology is bringing features like__________, virtual reality elements, photo editor.
4. __________ that you see in your timeline along with the notifications that you receive from these apps is curated mainly by AI.
5. Game such as PUBG or Fortnite essentially starts playing against a couple of __________ and then move to play against real players in consecutive levels.

C. ANSWER THE FOLLOWING QUESTIONS.

1. Give any two examples of real life where you have observed that AI is helping you.

   ____

   ____

2. Define the term smart search on web.

   ____

   ____

3. Give any two examples of AI helping in the field of communication.

4. Write any two key elements needed to design a poster for job advertisement.

5. Write the functionality of Google AI.

Notes

Quiz Card

TICK THE CORRECT ANSWER.

1. __________ is not the required property of Knowledge representation.
   a. Inferential Efficiency
   b. Inferential Adequacy
   c. Representational Verification
   d. Representational Adequacy
2. An AI agent perceives and acts upon the environment using__________.
   a. Sensors
   b. Actuators
   c. Algorithm
   d. Data
3. The exploration problem is where __________.
   a. Agent have the knowledge of State and actions
   b. Agent does not have the knowledge of State and actions
   c. Only actions are known to the agent
   d. Only knowledge are known to the agent
4. __________ is used to build complex sentences in knowledge representation.
   a. Symbols
   b. Connectives
   c. Quantifier
   d. Determiner
5. Automatic Reasoning tool is used in __________.
   a. Personal Computers
   b. Microcomputers
   c. LISP Machines
   d. Macro computer
6. __________ makes two different Logical expressions look identical.
   a. Unification
   b. Lifting
   c. Inference Process
   d. Intersect Process
7. Web Crawler is an example of __________.
   a. Intelligent Agent
   b. Problem-solving agent
   c. Simple reflex agent
   d. Model-based agent
8. The main function of problem-solving agent is to __________.
   a. Solve the given problem
   b. Reach the goal
   c. Solve the given problem and reach the goal
   d. Find out which sequence of action will get it to the goal state.
9. A knowledge-based agent can be defined with __________ levels.
   a. 1 Levels
   b. 2 Levels
   c. 3 Levels
   d. 4 Levels
10. Ways to achieve AI in real-life are __________.
    a. Machine Learning
    b. Deep Learning
    c. Both a & b
    d. None of the above

3 AI ETHICS

Structure Bot

In this chapter, we will discuss:

- The meaning of the term Ethical Issues
- Complexities of concepts surrounding ethics (bias, access, privacy) in AI
- AI bias and AI access

Objective Bot

At the end of this chapter, you should be able to:

- Know how the emerging trends in different fields are getting affected by AI
- Understand the implications of AI
- Know the ethical issues around AI

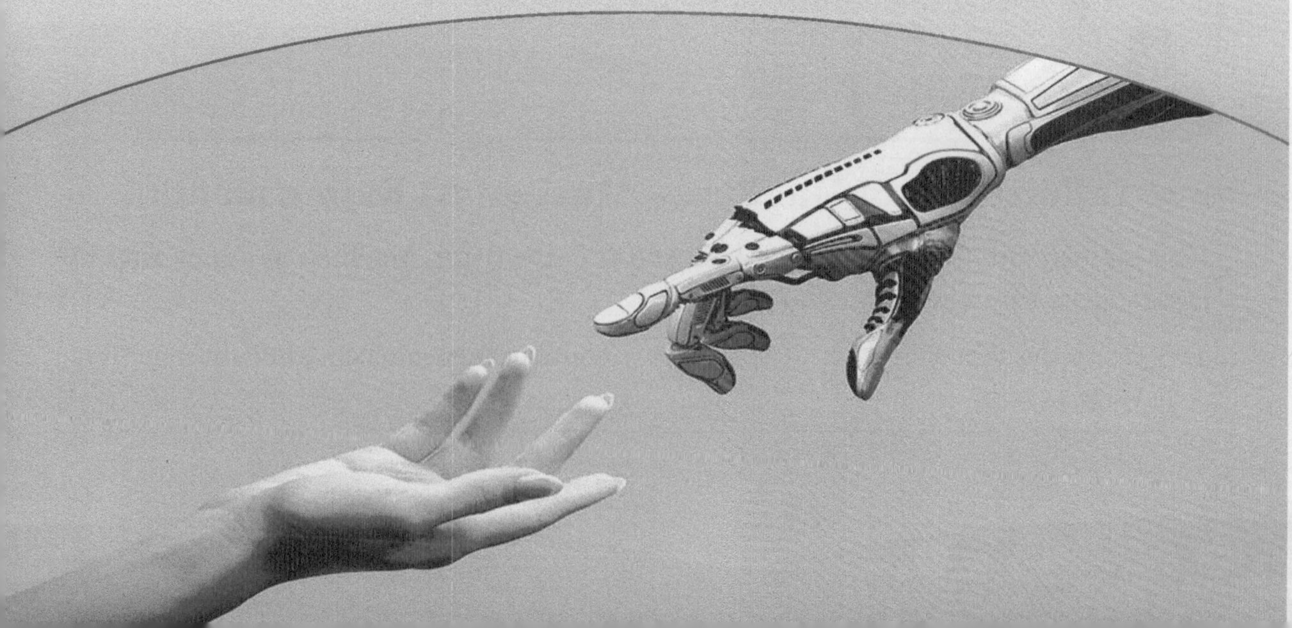

Introduction

Artificial Intelligence applications have many provisions to communicate with various other technologies which are useful to users with visual impairments.

AI Apps provides:

- AI expanded microscopes, for pathologists for real-time detection of cancer.
- Help people with visual impairments to use the touch feature to explore the objects.

Recent technologies such as AI-based chat bots, Google Assistant, Siri, Alexa provide interactions by using **Natural Language Processing** in interpreting the user questions by providing meaningful solutions.

Till now, we have learned to identify and appreciate Artificial Intelligence and describe its applications in our daily lives. In this chapter, we will know about the ethical issues surrounding AI and their societal impact.

Fact Bot

AI is already in Movies such as, "Jarvis," "Vision" from Avengers, or "The Terminator" are all part of the AI world in movies.

Activity I

Infinite Drum Machine – Musical AI Experiments

It is built by the Google Creative Lab, the Infinite Drum Machine is a new way to create beats using everyday sounds.

1. Go to the following link: https://experiments.withgoogle.com/ai/drum-machine/view/

2. Following screen appears, and click on start playing.

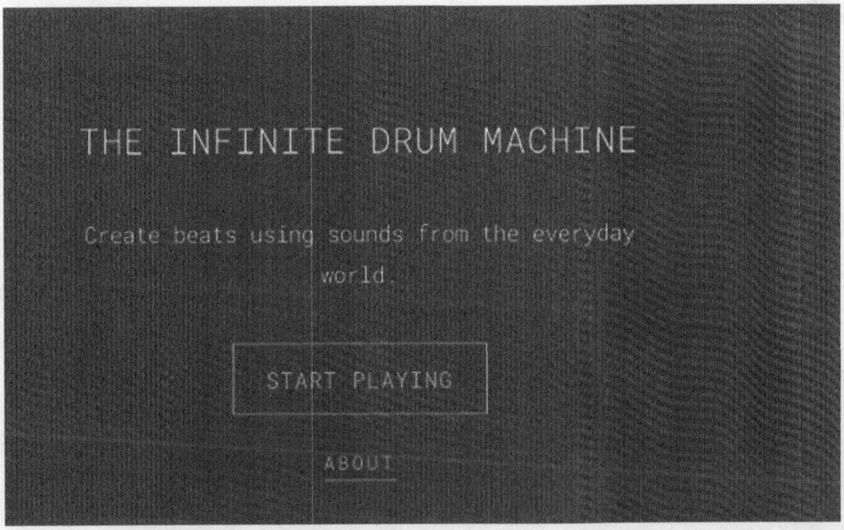

3. Click on the circle given, once you click they will get highlighted and the beat is added to the list of beats to play.
4. Once you select the beats/highlighted the circle, click on Play button.

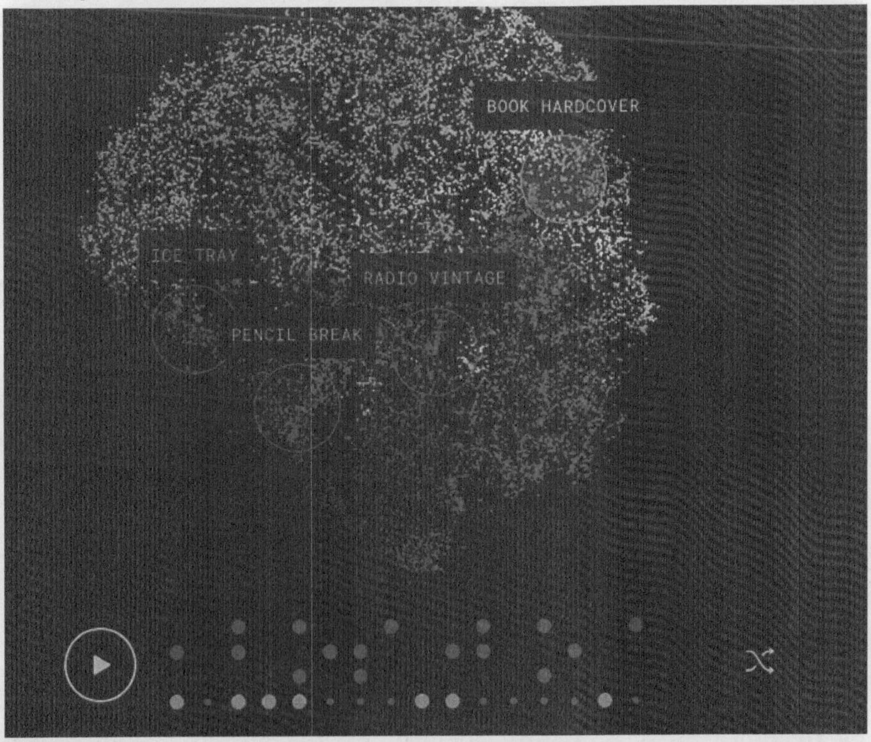

5. The drum will start playing on the beats you have selected.

AI Ethics

Artificial Intelligence ethics, or AI ethics, comprise of a set of values, principles, and techniques which employ widely accepted standards of right and wrong to guide moral conduct in the development and deployment of Artificial Intelligence technologies.

Ethics can be defined as:

- The study of values.
- Generating moral values for good or bad, right or wrong.

Ethics plays a major role in scientific researches (stem cell research, cloning/genetically modified food, nuclear technology).

Myths prevailing around the concept of AI ethics are:

- Loss of job due to automation.
- We either get too much or too little leisure time.
- Loss of sense of being unique.
- Lose of privacy rights.
- The accomplishment of AI will mean the end of the human race

AI ethics and safety must be a priority in the design and implementation of AI systems. AI Ethics emerges to avoid individual and societal harms which are caused by the misuse, abuse, poor design, or unintended negative consequences of AI systems.

Definition

Ethics can be defined as the study of values, generating moral values for good and bad, right, and wrong.

Robot ethics/ Roboethics

Robot ethics can be defined as Morality of how human's constructs, design, use and treat robots and other artificially intelligent created beings.

"Robot rights" is the concept that people must have some moral obligations towards the machines which is created artificially intelligent, similar to human rights or animal rights. Robot rights, such as a right to exist and perform its own mission, can be linked to the robot duty to serve human being, by linking it with human rights to human duties before society.

Robot ethics include:

- Right to life and liberty
- Freedom of thought, expression
- Equality before the law

Threat to Human Dignity

AI technology should never be used to replace the people in the positions which require respect and care. Position which AI cannot or should nor replace humans are:

- A customer service representative (AI technology is currently being used for telephone-based interactive voice response systems)
- A therapist
- A soldier
- A judge
- A police officer

Tip Bot

Robot rights are the concept according to which people must have moral obligations towards their machines.

Activity II

Tic-Tac-Toe game

Tic-tac-toe: noughts and crosses or Xs and Os, is a paper-and-pencil game for two players, X and O. In this player play turn by turn, and mark the spaces in a 3×3 grid. The player who succeeds in placing three of their marks in a diagonal, horizontal, or vertical row is the winner. It is a solved game with a forced draw assuming best play from both players

GamePlay:

To win the game, a player must place three of their marks in a horizontal, vertical, or diagonal row.

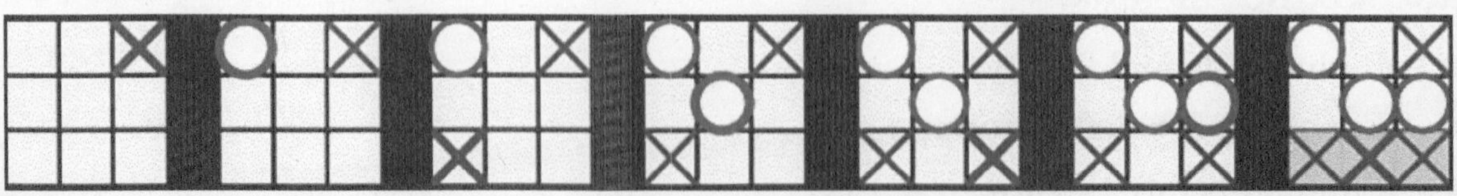

1. Go to the following link: https://playtictactoe.org/
2. The following page appears:

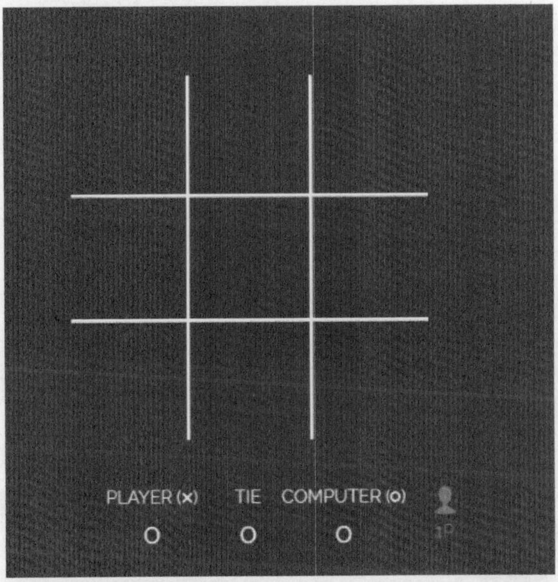

3. Start playing the game and try to mark the three X's in horizontal, vertical or diagonal row, similarly your opponent (computer in this case) also try to mark its 0's to win the game.

4. In case, if nobody makes horizontal, vertical or diagonal row, the game get Tie.

What actually AI is?

Artificial Intelligence is a form of technique or technology through which computers are able to perform cognitive tasks which was earlier performed by humans. Working on data, making sense of data up to a point where they could help us make decisions.

Approaches among AI

- AI focuses on data-based AI, in these algorithms are written to work with AI and further to interpret the data.
- Knowledge-based approach (expert systems) and context-based approach (pattern recognition, image recognition, and speech recognition); where matched data could be placed in different categories.

AI bias or Machine Learning Bias

Phenomenon which occurs when an algorithm produces a discriminatory result due to incorrect assumptions.

Memory Bot

Today AI technology is used for telephone based interactive response system.

Aim of AI is to provide an ease of access to various AI technology, which are socially beneficial, fair, accountable, and will works for everyone while solving humanitarian and environmental challenges.

Artificial Intelligence provides immense potential to gather, analyze, and combine the vast quantities of data from various sources with privacy.

AI privacy

One's ability to control the digital data in terms of how it is stored, modified, and exchanged between the different parties.

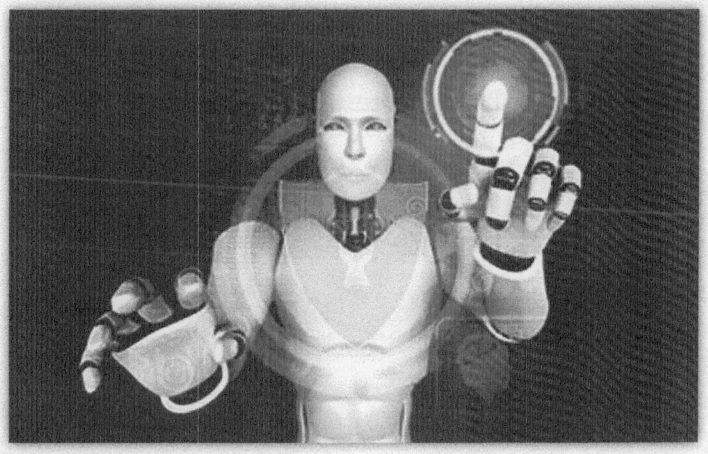

Check your Progress - I

State whether the following statements are True or False.

a. Ethics can be defined as the study of values, generating moral values for good and bad, right, and wrong. True/False

b. Robot ethics can be defined as morality of how human's constructs, design, use and treat robots and other artificially intelligent created beings. True/False

c. Artificial Intelligence is a form of technique or technology through which computers are not able to perform cognitive tasks which was earlier performed by humans. True/False

Answer: True, True, False.

Artificial Intelligence: Boon or Bane

AI focuses on the data-based approach (Pattern recognition, Image recognition, and Speech recognition).

Human Intelligence has made the machine to think critically and assist humans to take all the important decisions. The machine uses algorithms, to get the best matched results on the basis of data which is entered as an input to the machine.

AI technology is helping a lot in human lives for making the life better, but a small mistake can lead to a negative result and potentially create problems.

Artificial Intelligence (AI) Pros:

- **AI machine:**
  - Doesn't get tired.
  - Can take rational decisions.
  - Can be used in Health Care, Security, Education, Entertainment, Transport.
  - Gives accurate and fast results.

Artificial Intelligence (AI) Cons:

- AI technology is costly.
- AI machine lacks in creativity and emotions.
- Privacy.
- Legal malpractices.

DEFINITION

AI privacy is defined as one's ability to control the digital data in terms of how it is stored, modified, and exchanged between the different parties.

Activity III

pix2pix – Image to image translation

You can now can turn simple line drawings into beautiful works of art. Sketch a simple line drawing and watch the pix2pix AI automatically transform your creation into cats, buildings or shoes.

1. Go to the link: https://affinelayer.com/pixsrv/
2. The following screen appears:

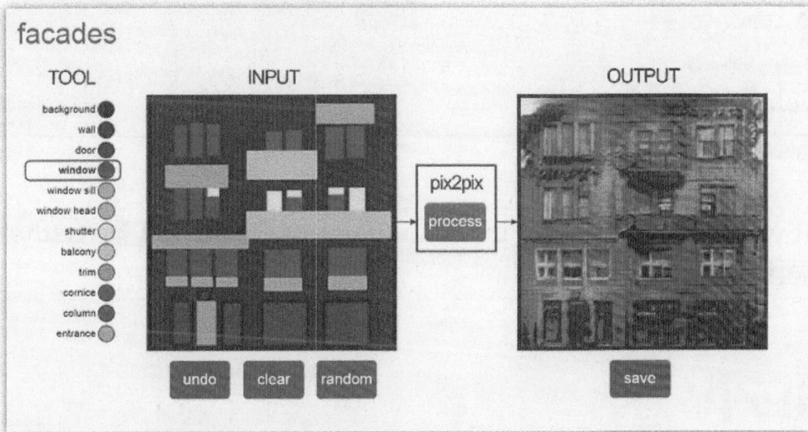

3. Click on clear and blank input screen will appear. You can see in the left side Tools are given. Select the tool of your choice.
4. In this we have selected Windows and draw two windows, balcony and door.
5. Once your drawing gets completed, click on process.

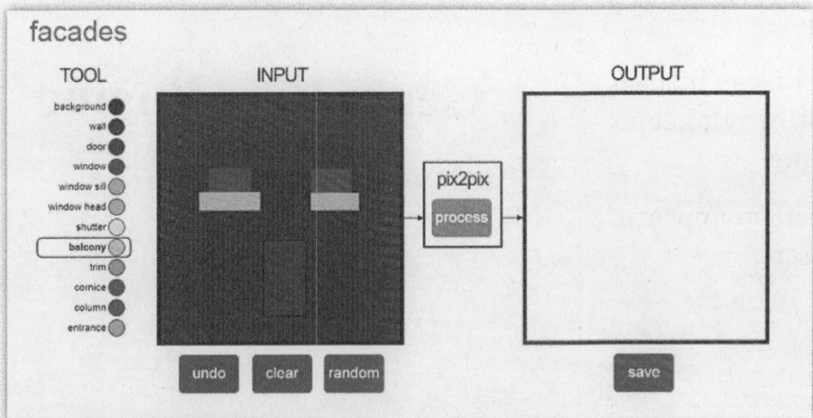

6. It will take few seconds to download the model.
7. You will see the output of your model in the output screen.

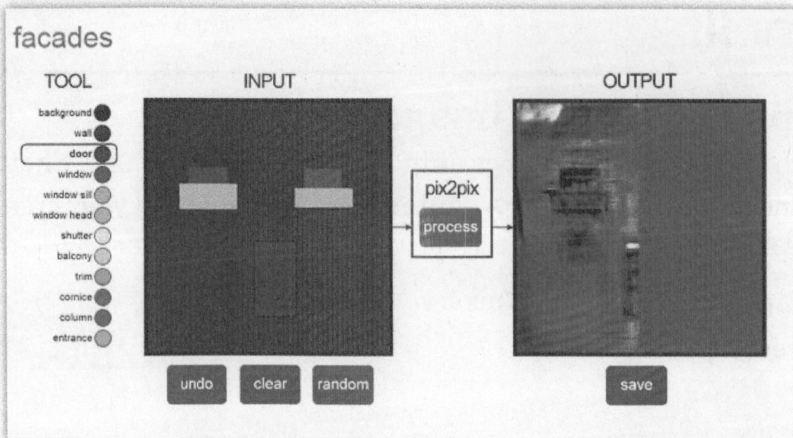

8. To save the model, click on the save.

Fact Bot

AI can Write, A robot wrote an article on an earthquake in California by gathering data from a seismograph.

Activity IV

AttnGAN – Image generation machine

It's a storytelling machine that automatically generates synthetic images as you write new words and sentences. It's part of a larger project, Runway that enables AI to be used creatively.

1. Go to the link: https://experiments.runwayml.com/generative_engine/
2. The following screen appears, Click on Let's start.

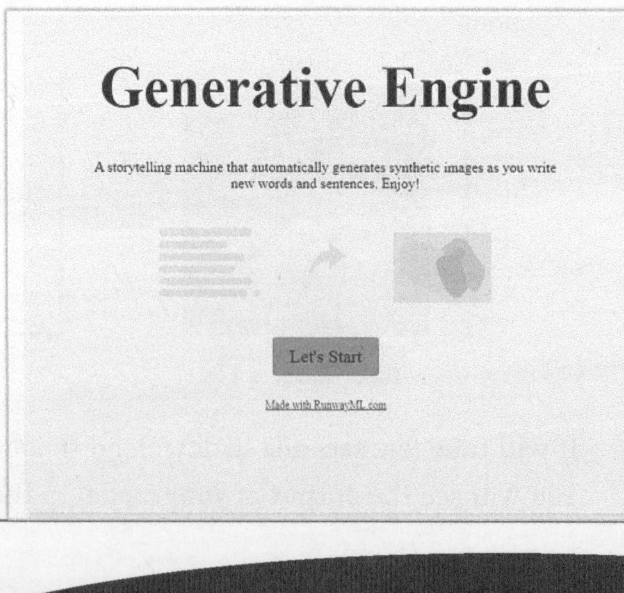

3. Next Screen appears, Write the following text:

    a beautiful morning

    sun is rising

    room with curtains sun rays are coming inside the room

    wake up early

    books in the room

    studying Artificial intelligence

    Click on the PlayBack.

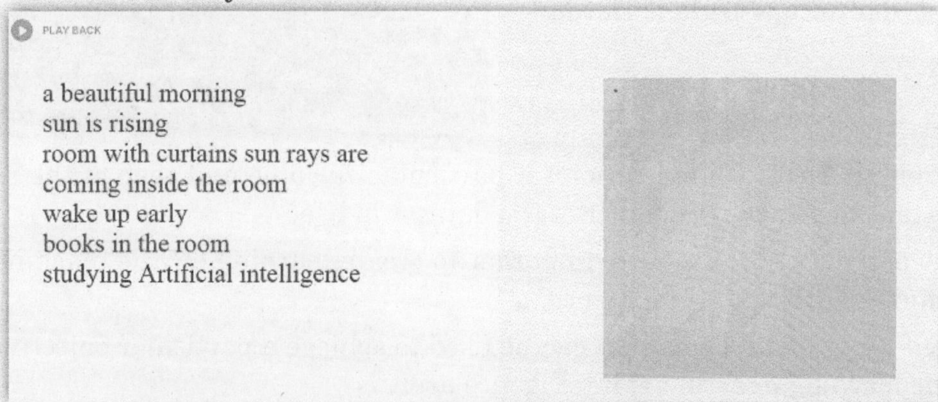

4. You will see the synthetic images are creating and images are changing as per the text given.

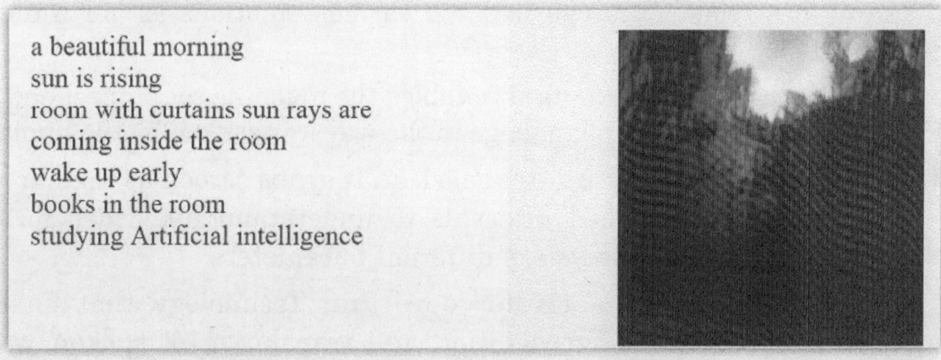

5. So, you can see that it is very easy to do storytelling.

Tip Bot

The earliest instance of #AI; is the golden robots which was created by the Greek god Hephaestus to help him to move around.

Extra Byte

DATA AND DATA SETS

Data

- Data can be defined as the collection of facts and statistics which is used either for reference or for analysis of the data.
- The singular form of Data is Datum.

Dataset

- A data set is a collection or a group of data wherein every column denotes a particular variable and each of the rows will pertain to a specific member of the dataset in use.
- The use of a data set is required in order to create learning for the machine in the context of Artificial Intelligence.
- Different kinds of data sets that can be used to achieve a particular objective in machine learning in artificial intelligence are:
  - o **Image Processing:** Data sets for image processing can be used for object captioning, detection and segmentation of the dataset.
  - o **Sentiment Analysis:** It categorizes the various emotions as per the type and its intensity.
  - o **Natural Language Processing:** It enables the machine to comprehend the human language in the way it is spoken by the humans.

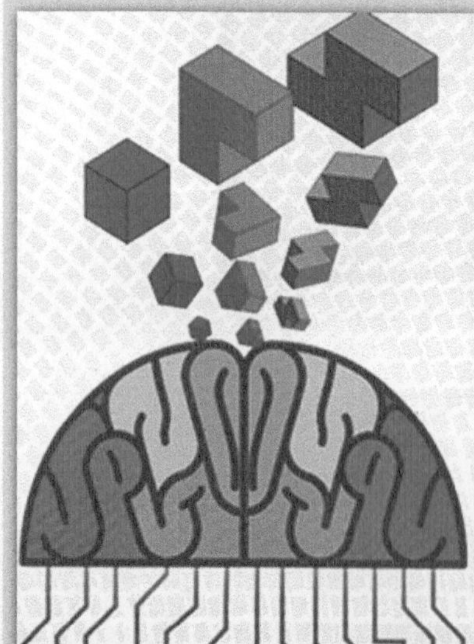

  - o **Video Processing:** It grabs screen at regular and timed intervals to understand live video for the analysis of different parameters.
  - o **Speech Recognition:** Technology that enables the recognition and translation of spoken words into text by the machines.
  - o **Internet of Things (IoT):** Countless objects which we use in our day-to-day lives in order to run them as smoothly as we can. These devices tend to rely on the internet to run the readings and gather data from responsible sources and provide digital intelligence.

Check your Progress - II

Fill in the Blanks.

a. AI focuses on the _______ approach.

b. Human Intelligence has made the machine to _________ humans to take all the important decisions.

c. _________ is helping a lot in human lives for making the life better, but a small mistake can lead to a negative result and potentially create problems.

Answer: data-based, think and assist, AI technology

Balloon Debate

A balloon debate is a debate in which a number of speakers attempt to win after the approval of an audience. The audience is invited to imagine that the speakers are flying in a hot-air balloon which is sinking and that someone must be thrown out if everyone is not to die.

Each speaker has to explain why they should not be thrown out of the balloon to save the remaining one. Typically each participant speaks on behalf of a famous person, profession, fictional character, and other perilous situations may take the place of the sinking balloon.

Visualization: All the speakers are flying in a hot-air balloon which is about to sink. You need to take the decision about who should be thrown out so that no one will die.

Attempt: To encourage all the participants to argue why they shouldn't be thrown out of the balloon.

DEFINITION

Balloon Debate is a debate or sharing of ideas and facts among the presenters who debate to win the audience approval.

Activity V

Overview:

Activity introduces students the concepts which they will use in formal debates, such as making initial speeches, giving responses to questions, and addressing other people's arguments.

Task:

- Select four students to take part in the debate.
- Ask them to think of a character (or you can assign them, if you prefer).
- Set a theme for the character, e.g. "a historical figure", "a modern celebrity", "someone you admire", etc.

Scenario:

- These four students are in a hot air balloon. It is sinking as it is too heavy. The only way for them to survive is one person to be thrown out of the balloon.
- In the first round each person has to give a short speech of less than 2 minutes (short as 30 seconds) explaining why they should not be thrown out of the balloon.
- Second round deals with questions and answers. Ask each student one question such as:
    a. Why is your character special?
    b. What is the best thing about your character?
    c. Can you tell us about your character's job?
    d. Can you tell us a story that shows why your character is special?
    e. Can you give more detail about a point in your speech?
- Students should get a reasonable time to answer but they will be stop if they take too long time.
- Ask a second question of each if there is time.
- Now ask the class to vote on who persuaded them most.

Note: For a more competitive atmosphere you can hold a vote between each round for which character gets "thrown out of the balloon" and joins the audience.

Tip Bot

Elon Musk is worried about the impact of #AI on humanity. He founded Neuralink and created a devices that could link human brains with computers.

Activity VI

Talk to Books – Intelligent conversation

Google Research has developed multiple activities to teach AI the art of human conversation. In Talk to Books, you can type any statement or a question, and the model will scan over 100,000 books to find a variety of responses based on your input.

1. Visit the link: https://books.google.com/talktobooks/
2. The following screen appears:

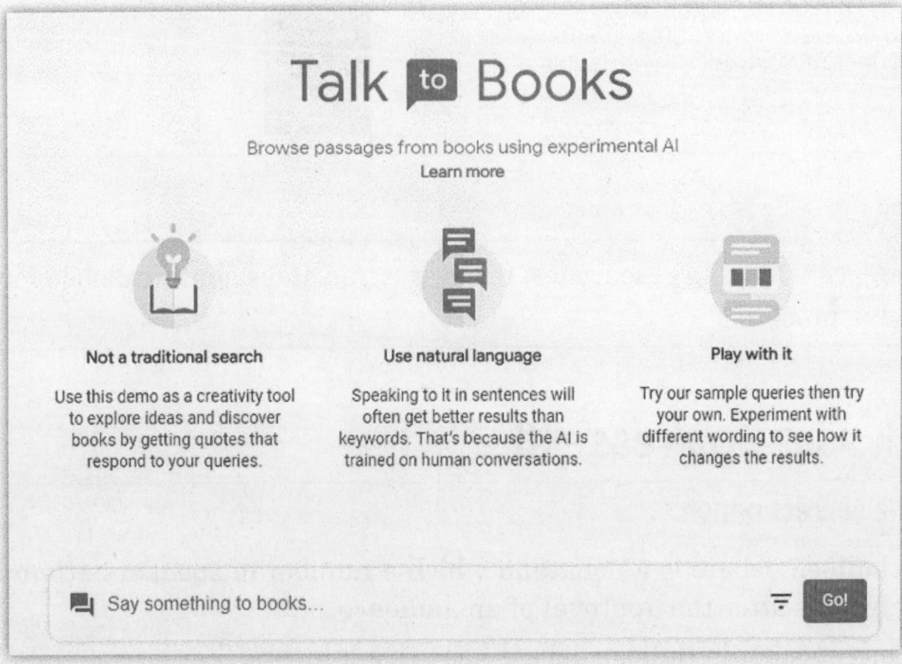

3. Write: "Emoji Scavenger Hunt is a browser-based game built with machine learning and uses your phone's camera and a neural network to try and guess what it's seeing." Text in the space (Sy something to books...) given.

4. Click on GO.

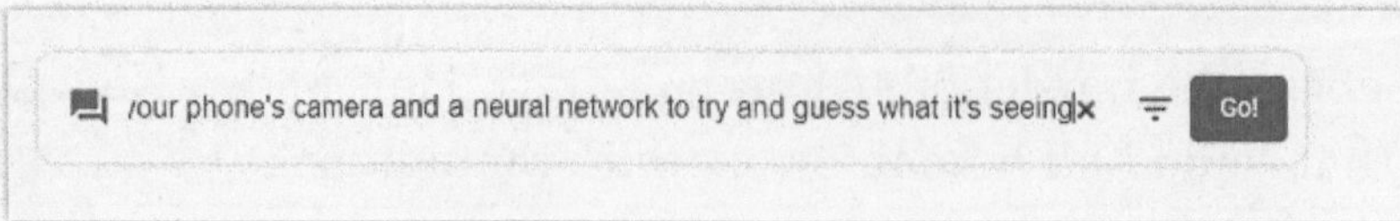

5. You will get a list of books, which contains the passage searched.

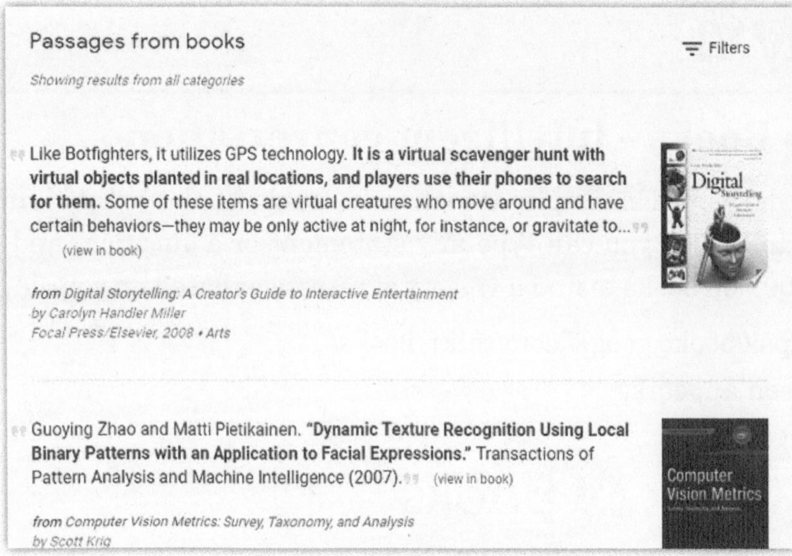

Memory Bot

AI inclusion suggests making researches, tools, systems and scientific developments available to solve problems.

Check your Progress - III

Tick the correct option.

a. A balloon debate is a debate in which a number of speakers attempt to **win/loss** after the approval of an audience.

b. Each speaker in Balloon debate has to explain why they **should/ should not** be thrown out of the balloon to save the remaining.

c. Aim of AI is **to provide/not to provide** an ease of access to various AI technology which are socially beneficial.

Answer: win, should, to provide.

TECH BOT

- **Artificial Intelligence ethics:** It comprise of a set of values, principles, and techniques which employ widely accepted standards of right and wrong to guide moral conduct in the development and deployment of Artificial Intelligence technologies.
- **Robot ethics:** Morality of how human's constructs, design, use and treat robots and other artificially intelligent created beings.
- **AI privacy:** One's ability to control the digital data in terms of how it is stored, modified, and exchanged between the different parties.

Recap Bot

- Artificial Intelligence ethics comprise of a set of values, principles, and techniques which employ widely accepted standards of right and wrong to guide moral conduct in the development and deployment of Artificial Intelligence technologies.
- Recent technologies such as AI-based chat bots, Google Assistant, Siri, Alexa provide interactions by using **Natural Language Processing** in interpreting the user questions by providing meaningful solutions.
- AI Ethics can be defined as:
  - The study of values
  - Generating moral values for good or bad, right or wrong.
- Robot ethics can be defined as Morality of how human's constructs, design, use and treat robots and other artificially intelligent created beings.
- Artificial Intelligence is a form of technique or technology through which computers are able to perform cognitive tasks which was earlier performed by humans.
- **AI bias or Machine Learning bias** is a phenomenon which occurs when an algorithm produces a discriminatory result due to incorrect assumptions.
- **AI privacy** is defined as one's ability to control the digital data in terms of how it is stored, modified, and exchanged between the different parties.
- AI focuses on the data-based approach (Pattern recognition, Image recognition, and Speech recognition).
- Human Intelligence has made the machine to think critically and assist humans to take all the important decisions. The machine uses algorithms, to get the best matched results on the basis of data which is entered as an input to the machine.
- Balloon Debate is a debate or sharing of ideas and facts among the presenters who debate to win the audience approval.

Brain Bot

A. MULTIPLE CHOICE QUESTIONS.

1. An Artificial Intelligence application provides:
   a. AI expanded microscopes ☐
   b. Visual impairments device with touch feature to explore the objects ☐
   c. Both a and b ☐
   d. None of the above ☐
2. Recent technologies such as AI-based chatbots, Google Assistant, Siri, Alexa provide interactions by using:
   a. Natural Language Processing ☐
   b. Computer Vision ☐
   c. Data analytics ☐
   d. Data Science ☐
3. Artificial Intelligence ethics, or AI ethics, comprise of:
   a. a set of values ☐
   b. principles, techniques ☐
   c. accepted standards of right and wrong to guide moral conduct ☐
   d. All of the above ☐
4. AI Ethics plays a major role in:
   a. Scientific researches ☐ b. Mathematical research ☐
   c. Energy area research ☐ d. Material science ☐
5. Myths prevailing around the concept of AI ethics are:
   a. Loss of job due to automation ☐
   b. We either get too much or too little leisure time ☐
   c. Loss of sense of being unique ☐
   d. All of the above ☐

B. FILL IN THE BLANKS.

1. AI ethics and safety must be a priority in the design and implementation of________.
2. _______can be defined as Morality of how human's constructs, design, use and treat robots and other artificially intelligent created beings.
3. Robot ethics include _______and liberty.
4. Places which AI cannot or should nor replace ______are customer service representative, therapist, soldier, judge, police officer.
5. Artificial Intelligence is a form of technique or technology through which computers are able to perform _______ which was earlier performed by humans.

C. MATCH THE FOLLOWING.

Column A	Column B
1. Machine Learning bias	i. Pattern recognition
2. AI privacy	ii. Sharing of ideas and facts
3. Data-based approach	iii. Control the digital data
4. Balloon Debate	iv. Scientific developments available to solve problems
5. AI inclusion	v. Discriminatory result due to incorrect assumptions

D. ANSWER THE FOLLOWING QUESTIONS.

1. Define the term AI Ethics.

____

____

2. Explain any two applications areas where Robots are used.

____

____

3. Explain the term Robo Ethics.

____

____

4. Name a game where to win the game; a player must place three of their marks in a horizontal, vertical, or diagonal row.

____

____

5. What do you mean by AI bias or Machine Learning bias?

____

____

Lab Activity

AI Duet – An AI Experiment with a Piano

1. Go to the link: https://experiments.withgoogle.com/ai/ai-duet/view/
2. The following page appears, and click on PLAY:

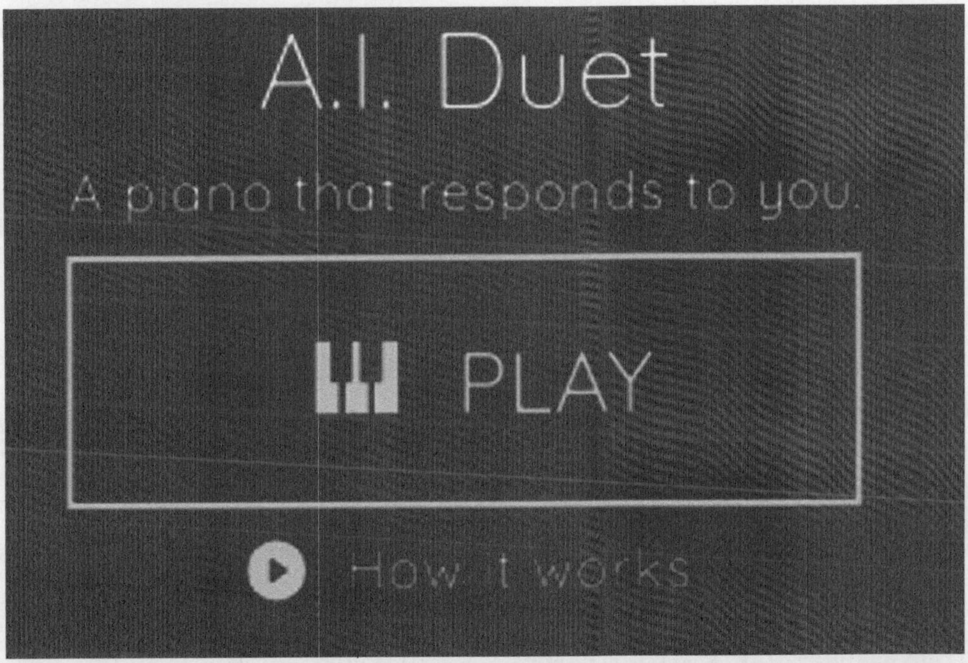

3. Now, press the keys of Piaono by clicking your mouse, using your computer keys, or even plugging into a MIDI keyboard, and the model will respond to your melody.

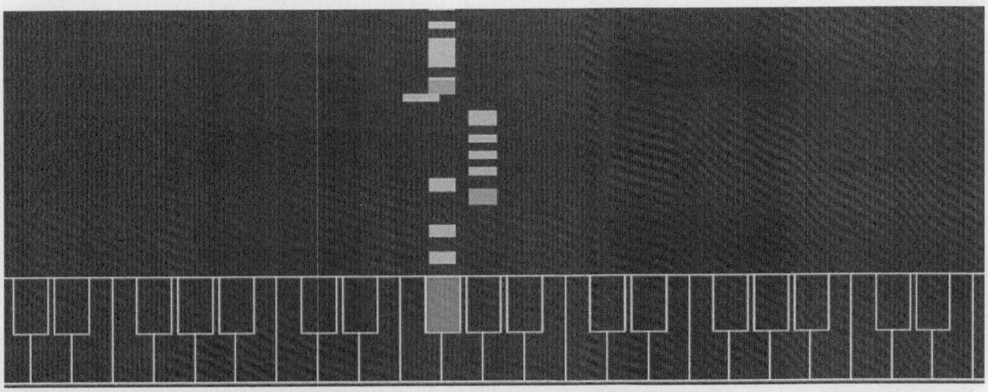

WORKSHEET

A. STATE WHETHER THE FOLLOWING STATEMENT ARE TRUE OR FALSE.

1. Working on data, making sense of data up to a point where they could help us make decisions. True/False
2. AI focuses on data-based AI, in which algorithms are written to work with AI and further to interpret the data. True/False
3. Knowledge-based approach includes the use of pattern recognition. True/False
4. Context-based approach includes pattern recognition, image recognition, and speech recognition. True/False
5. AI bias or Machine Learning bias is a phenomenon which occurs when an algorithm produces a correct result due to incorrect assumptions. True/False

B. FILL IN THE BLANKS.

1. Aim of AI is to provide an ________ to various AI technology.
2. Artificial Intelligence provides immense potential to gather, analyze, and combine the vast quantities of data from various sources with______.
3. AI privacy is one's ability to control the ______ in terms of how it is stored, modified, and exchanged between the different parties.
4. AI focuses on the ________ approach which Speech recognition.
5. ________ has made the machine to think critically and assist humans to take all the important decisions.

C. ANSWER THE FOLLOWING QUESTIONS.

1. Name the approaches used among Artificial Intelligence.
2. Write any two advantages and disadvantages of AI.

3. Define the term Balloon debate.

4. Explain the aim of AI.

5. How human intelligence is helpful in AI?

Notes

Quiz Card

TICK THE CORRECT ANSWER.

1. Applications of Artificial Intelligence are:
   a. Expert Systems b. Vision System
   c. Gaming d. All of the above
2. If a robot changes its own trajectory as per the external conditions, then the robot is __
   a. Mobile b. Computer
   c. Intelligent d. Dump
3. ____________ language is not commonly used for AI?
   a. Python b. Perl
   c. LISP d. PROLOG
4. Most preferred language for AI and Machine learning is:
   a. Python b. Perl
   c. LISP d. PROLOG
5. Most preferred language for AI innovation is:
   a. Python b. Perl
   c. LISP d. PROLOG
6. Technique which was developed to determine whether a machine could or could not demonstrate the artificial intelligence is:
   a. Data Science b. Boolean Algebra
   c. Turing Test d. Algorithm
7. In the year 1950, Alan Turing introduced a test which is used to determine whether a machine can think like a human or not, and the test is known as:
   a. Turing Test b. Turning Test
   c. Testing Test d. Tunnel Test
8. Turing Test was based on:
   a. Imitation game b. Data game
   c. Pattern recognition d. Speech recognition
9. The component of an Expert system is________.
   a. Inference Engine b. Knowledge Base
   c. User Interface d. All of the above
10. Expert system is a part of AI which is used to solve complex problems, and to give the decision-making ability like human, with the help of:
    a. Knowledge base b. Inference engine
    c. User interface d. All of the above

PROJECT

Repeat until main button
Forward 10 normal
Look Right 90
Ask What is your name?
Say STEAM

PictoBlox

- PictoBlox is a Scratch 3.0-based graphical programming software.
- It is an ideal companion for the setting the first step into the world of programming.
- Its user-friendly interface and drag-and-drop functionality eliminate the need to memorize syntax and rules.
- In this we only require to focus on the problem at hand and develop skills such as logical reasoning and problem-solving.

To download PictoBlox

1. Visit the link: https://thestempedia.com/product/pictoblox/
2. Click on Download.

3. The following screen appears:

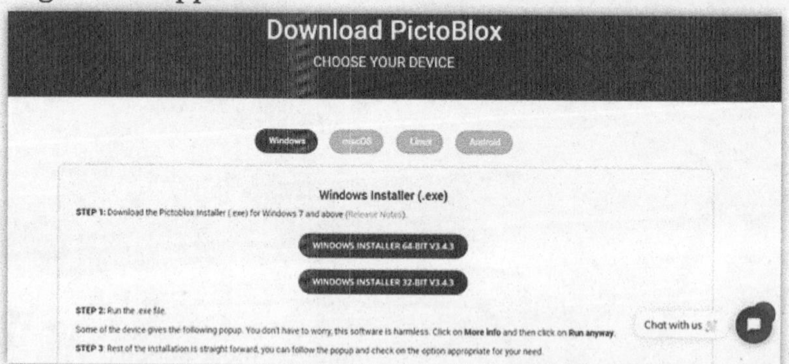

4. Choose your operating system. In this we have chosen Windows; and click on the WINDOWS INSTALLER 64-BITV3.4.3.
5. The next appears, ask you to enter your name and e-mail address, you can enter the required information and click on next. Or you can choose the option as No, thanks i just want to download the PictoBlox.

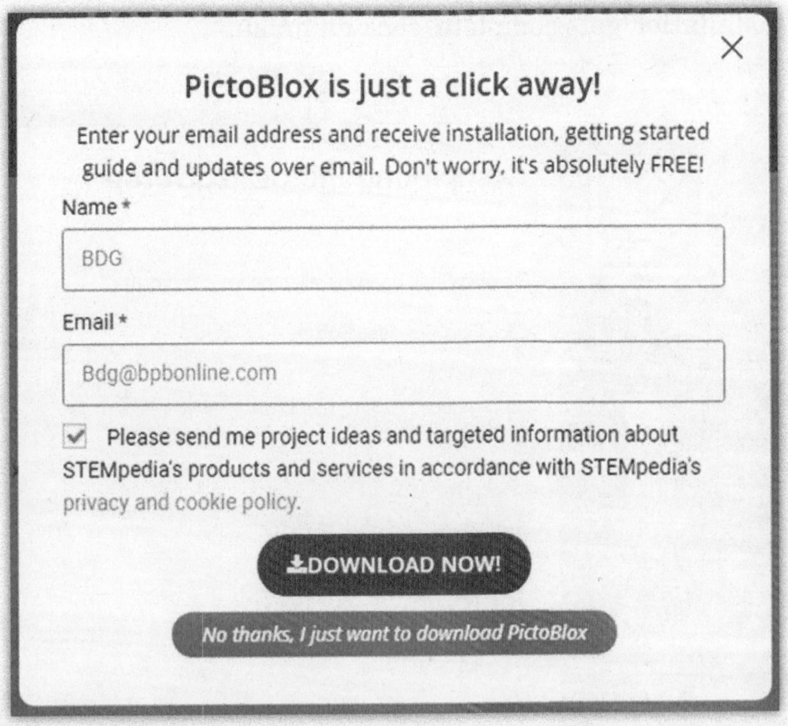

6. After this the software starts downloading.
7. Once it get downloaded, click on setup file to run the exe file.
8. It will start installing the software, and ask you for the location to save the file.
9. Click on install.

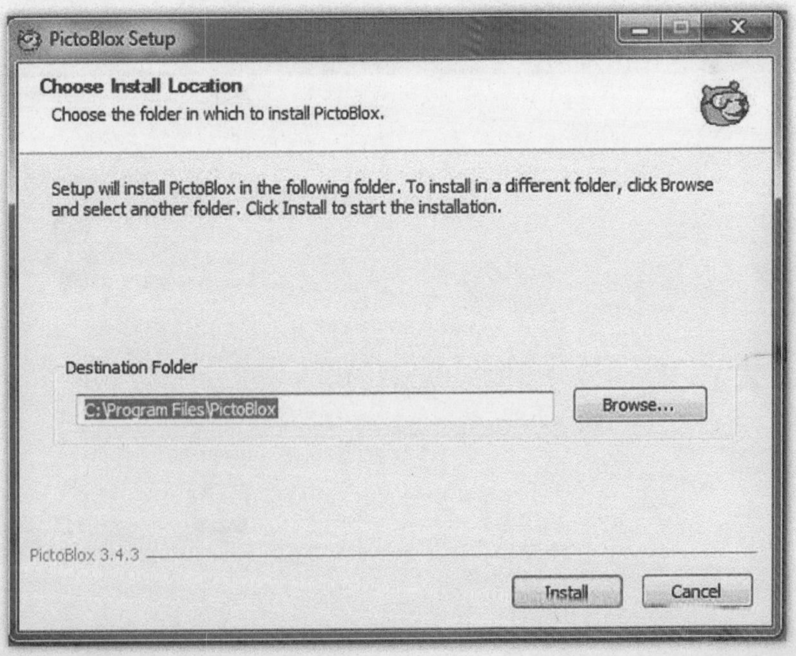

10. Once the installation gets complete, click on finish.

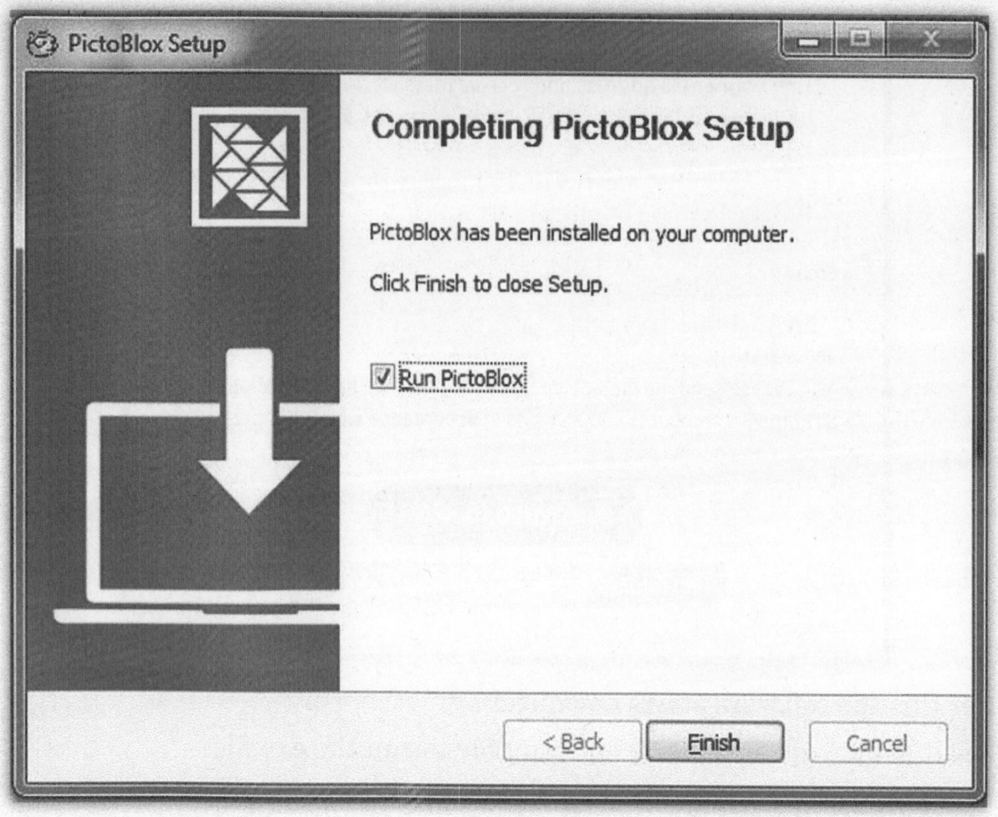

11. Click on the PictoBlox icon, the following screen appears:

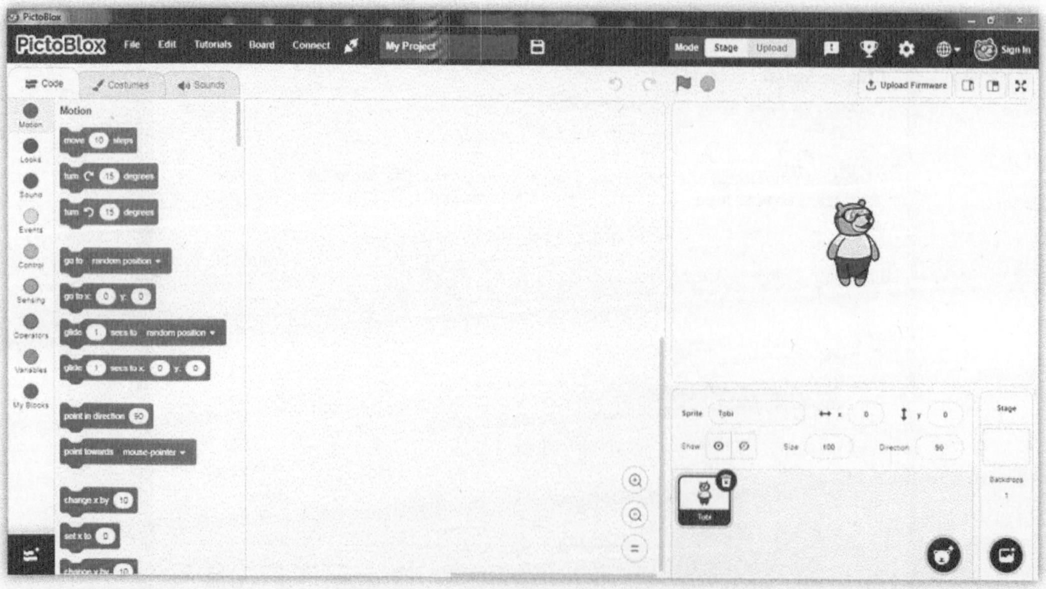

PictoBlox, like Scratch, has the following basic elements:

◆ **Sprites**

A sprite is an object, or a character, which performs different actions in the projects.

◆ **Stage**

The stage is the area where the sprite performs actions according to your program.

◆ **Script**

A script is a program or a code in PictoBlox/Scratch lingo. It is a set of 'blocks' that are arranged below one another in a specific order to perform a task or a series of tasks.

◆ **Blocks**

A block is like a jigsaw puzzle piece that is used to write programs by simply dragging and dropping them below one another in the scripting area.

◆ **Block Palette**

The block palette is under the Code tab. It consists of different palettes such as Motion, Sound, and Control.

Modes

PictoBlox has two modes:

1. **Stage Mode:** In this mode, you can write scripts for the sprite and boards like evive to interact with sprites in real-time. If you disconnect the board with Pictoblox, you cannot interact anymore.
2. **Upload Mode:** This mode allows you to write scripts and upload it to the board so that you can use even when it is not connected to your computer, for example, you need to upload a script for making moving robots.

Make your Own Smart AI Chabot Using Speech Recognition

We will make the chatbot which will recognize the speech and convert it into text using PictoBlox's Speech Recognition Extension and then answer the questions accordingly.

Step 1: Prerequisites to make the Chatbot

You need to have:

a. A laptop or a computer with a camera
b. The latest version of PictoBlox
c. A good Internet connection.

Step 2: Setting Up the Project

a. Open PictoBlox. (Download it from: https://thestempedia.com/product/pictoblox/)
b. Click on Board and select evive.

c. Click on the Add extension button and Select the Artificial Intelligence Extension.

d. Next, let's add the Text-to-speech extension, which will convert the Audio into a text message.

Step 3: Setting Up the Stage

Isaac

a. Let's add Isaac, the sprite which will be the character of our chatbot of our project, by clicking on Choose a Sprite button. A list of sprite will appear, Select **Isaac** from the library.

b. Now, let's add backdrop. Click on the **Choose a Backdrop** button and choose **Boardwalk** backdrop from the library.

Step 4: Writing the Script for AI Chatbot

Note: To execute the program **green flag** is clicked.

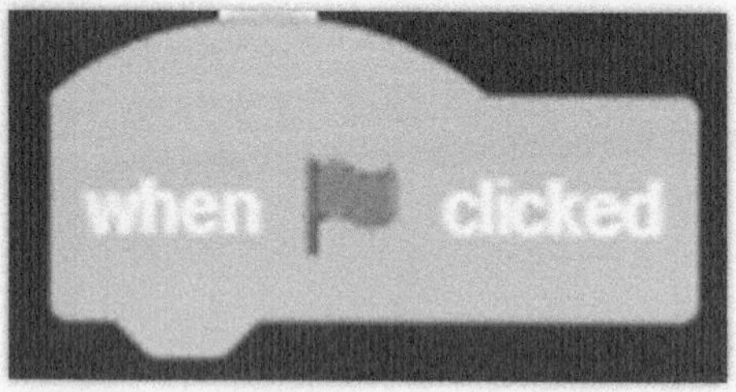

a. Get a speak () **block** from Text to Speech palette. This block will convert the text written in white space to audio form to be played on your PC/laptop speaker.

b. Write "Hello, I am Isaac your friend!" to introduce Isaac to the user.

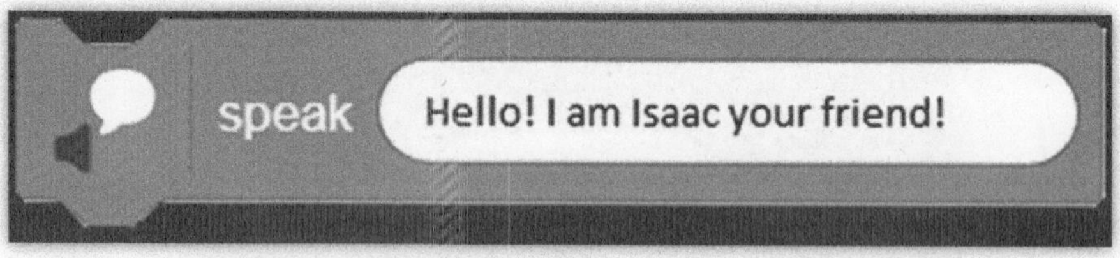

c. Again add a speak () block and ask for the user's name Write "What is your name?" into space given.

d. Add **recognize speech for () secs in ()** block from the *artificial intelligence* extension blocks. This block will records audio and sends it to the web to decode and convert the speech into the text form.

e. Now, the user's name is stored in the **speech recognition result** block. To use the user's name in further communication we will store it in a variable. Go to the Variables tab, click on **Make a New Variable** and make a **String** type variable named "**Name**" to store the name of the user.

f. Get a **set()** to () block from the Variables palette, select Name from the drop-down, and add speech recognition result inside it.

g. To make chatbot welcome users get a **speak()** block. Place a **join()** block inside it from the Operators palette.

h. Write "Welcome " into the first space of the join block.

i. Add the Name reporter block into the second space.

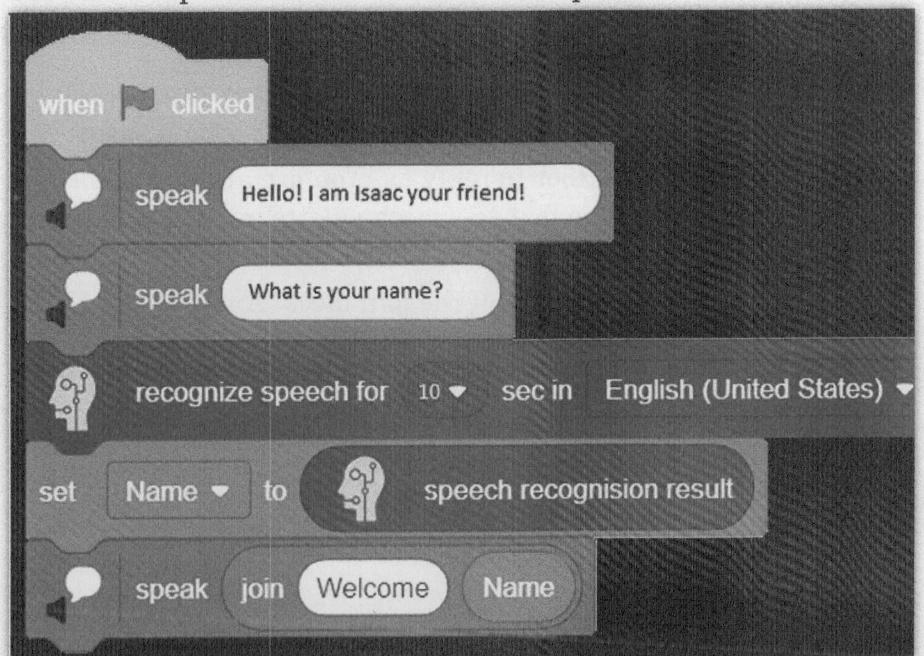

Chatting Up the Bot

a. To continuously chat with our chatbot, add in a forever block from the Controls block palette below the speak block.

b. Write "What's on your mind " into the first space of the join block.

c. And add the Name reporter block into the second space.

d. Now to again recognize the user's questions, add the recognize speech for () secs in () block from the artificial intelligence palette to record whatever the user is speaking.

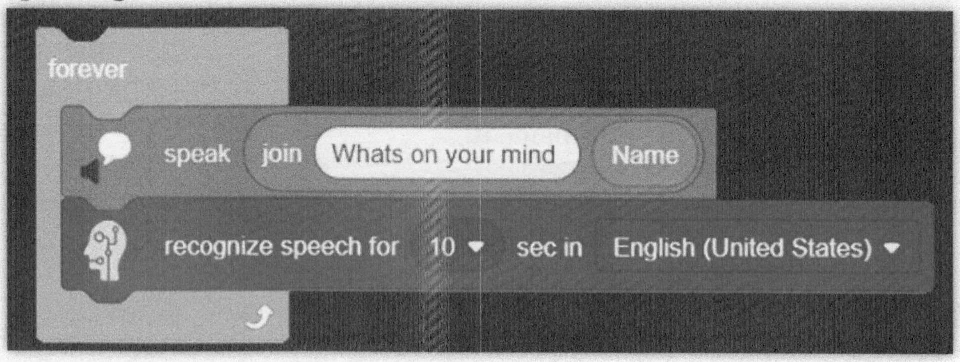

Adding the Questions and Answers

a. Add an if-else block from Controls block palette to check if recognized speech matches the question.

b. Inside the if arm, add an () = () block to check the result.

c. Now into the first blank space of equal to block, place, the speech recognition result block, and type in the question " Who am I? " in second space.

d. In this case we need, our chatbot to reply as "You are and the name of the user". So, add **speak()** block from the text-to-speech palette into the if portion and add a join () () block inside it from the operator's block palate.

e. Write "You are " into the first space of the join block. And add the Name reporter block into the second space.

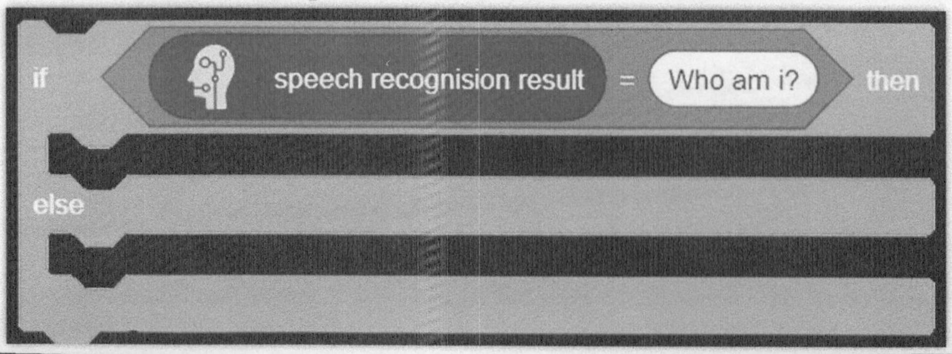

Note: You can add as many questions as you want.

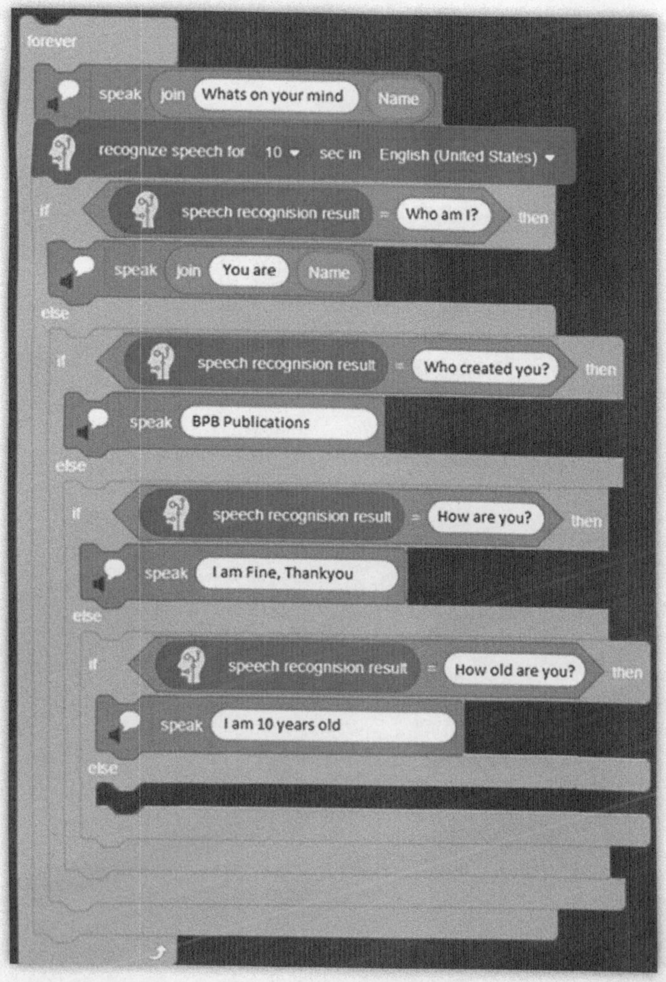

Adding the Default Case

If the recognized result does not match with any predefined questions then we will make Isaac say "Sorry! I don't understand it yet."

Add a **speak()** block into the last else arm of the question and write "Sorry! I don't understand it yet.".

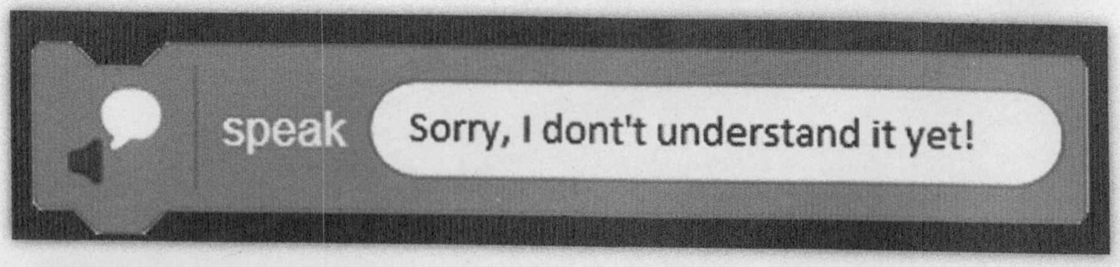

Code:

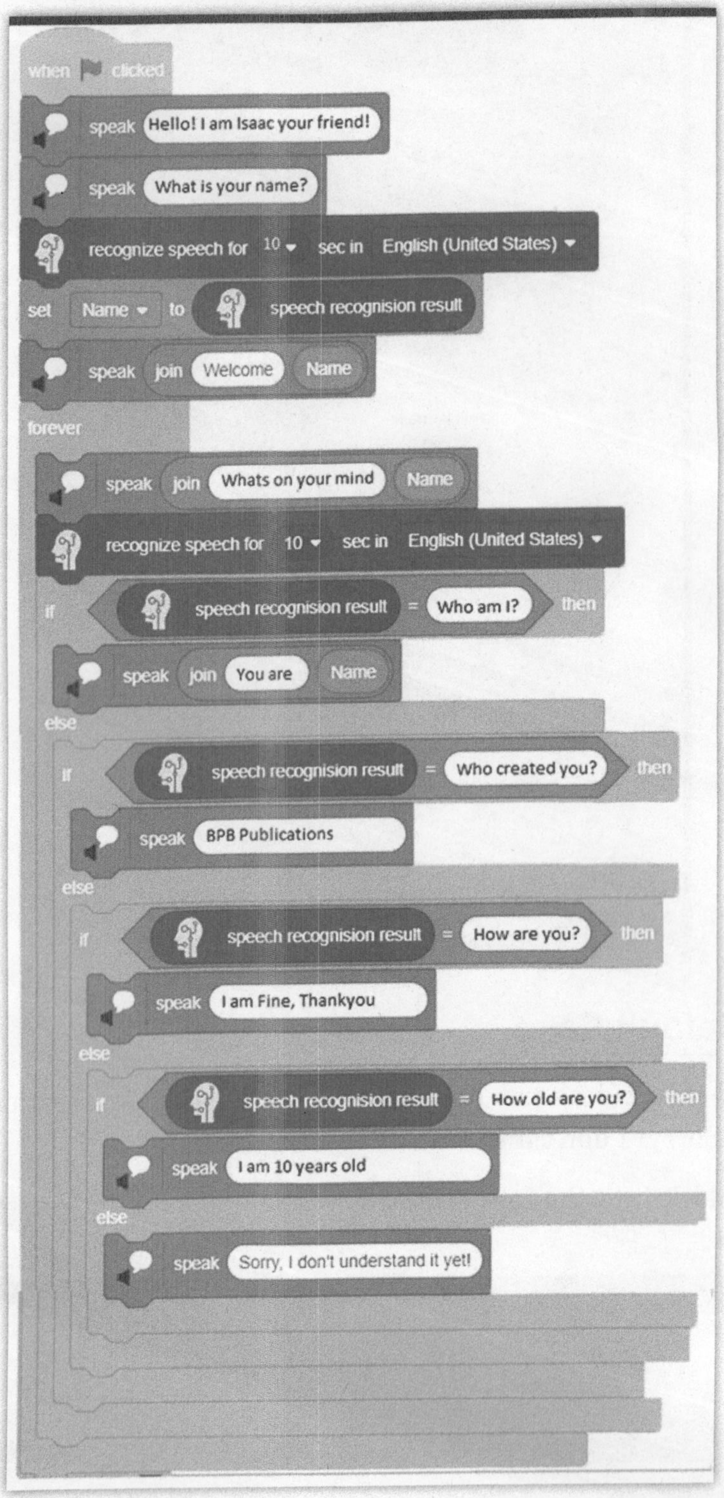
when clicked
speak Hello! I am Isaac your friend!
speak What is your name?
recognize speech for 10 sec in English (United States)
set Name to speech recognision result
speak join Welcome Name
forever
speak join Whats on your mind Name
recognize speech for 10 sec in English (United States)
if speech recognision result = Who am I? then
speak join You are Name
else
if speech recognision result = Who created you? then
speak BPB Publications
else
if speech recognision result = How are you? then
speak I am Fine, Thankyou
else
if speech recognision result = How old are you? then
speak I am 10 years old
else
speak Sorry, I don't understand it yet!

Sample Paper

Sample Paper

Time: 2 hours **Marks: 50**

A. Multiple choice questions. **1/2x10=5**

1. Artificial Intelligence is about_____.
   a. Playing a game on Computer
   b. Making a machine Intelligent
   c. Programming on Machine
   d. Putting your intelligence in Machine
2. Who is known as the -Father of AI"?
   a. Fisher Ada
   b. Alan Turing
   c. John McCarthy
   d. Allen Newell
3. The application/applications of Artificial Intelligence is/are
   a. Expert Systems
   b. Gaming
   c. Vision Systems
   d. All of the above
4. If a robot is able to change its own trajectory as per the external conditions, then the robot is:
   a. Mobile
   b. Non-Servo
   c. Open Loop
   d. Intelligent
5. Which of the given language is commonly used for AI?
   a. LISP
   b. C
   c. Java
   d. Perl
6. A technique used to determine whether a machine could or could not demonstrate the artificial intelligence is:
   a. Boolean Algebra
   b. Turing Test
   c. Logarithm
   d. Algorithm
7. The component of an Expert system is_________.
   a. Knowledge Base
   b. Inference Engine
   c. User Interface
   d. All of the above
8. AI agent perceives and acts upon the environment by using___.
   a. Sensors
   b. Perceiver
   c. Agents
   d. Machine
9. Web Crawler is an example of______.
   a. Intelligent Agent
   b. Problem-solving agent
   c. Simple reflex agent
   d. Model-based agent

10. The main function of problem-solving agent is to________.
   a. Solve the given problem and reach the goal
   b. Not to find out the sequence of action will get it to the goal state
   c. Find the state of the machine
   d. Find the problem.

B. Fill in the blanks. **1/2×10=5**

1. Artificial Intelligence, or 'AI', is the ____________ innovation for all the new age changes which are happening all around us.
2. Artificial intelligence initially was founded as an academic discipline in ____________.
3. AI field was founded on the assumption that human intelligence "can be so precisely described that a machine can be made to ____________ it".
4. Artificial Intelligence (AI) was first coined in 1956 at Dartmouth Conference by a cognitive scientist, ____________, at the Dartmouth Conference.
5. Artificial intelligence (AI) refers to the simulation of human intelligence in the machines which are ____________ to think like humans and mimic the actions of humans.
6. Artificial Intelligence can be applied to any machine which exhibits traits which are associated with a human mind such as learning and ____________.
7. Smart homes are homes that have all the electronic devices and security systems which are controlled by the owner with the ____________.
8. ____________ is the process of adding game-like components to a task to encourage the participation of user participation.
9. ____________ is a hand game which is played between two people, in which each player simultaneously forms one of three shapes with an outstretched hand.
10. Natural language processing (NLP) describes the interaction among the human language and ____________.

C. State whether the following statements are True or False. **1/2×10=5**

1. Mystery Animal is a new spin on the classic 20-questions game.

2. Emoji Scavenger Hunt is an interdisciplinary field that deals with how computers can be made to gain high-level understanding from digital images or videos.
3. Artificial Intelligence in daily life is used for Checking your schedules of daily task, Looking for directions (Google Map), Music and movie recommendations by digital assistants (Netflix).
4. Research is a process of systematic inquiry that entails collection of data.
5. A poster is a temporary promotion of an idea, product, or event which is put up in a public space for mass consumption.
6. Working on data, making sense of data up to a point where they could help us make decisions.
7. AI focuses on data-based AI, in which algorithms are written to work with AI and further to interpret the data.
8. Knowledge-based approach includes the use of pattern recognition.
9. Context-based approach includes pattern recognition, image recognition, and speech recognition.
10. AI bias or Machine Learning bias is a phenomenon which occurs when an algorithm produces a correct result due to incorrect assumptions.

D. Match the following. **1/2×10=5**

Column A	Column B
1. Chatbots	i. Python, Lisp
2. Applications of AI	ii. NLP
3. Mystery Animal	iii. Siri, Alexa
4. Programming language used in AI	iv. Computer Vision
5. Emoji Scavenger Hunt	v. Self-driving cars, chatbots
6. Pros of AI	vi. Increase in unemployment
7. IoT-enabled bands	vii. Expert system
8. AI in healthcare	viii. AI machines
9. Cons of AI	ix. Bulk of data with ease and work tirelessly
10. Lacks emotions	x. Helps physicians in diagnosis

E. Answer the following questions.

1. Write full forms for the following. 1×3=3

   a. NLP

   b. IoT

   c. AI

2. Define the following terms: 1×3=3

   a. Computer Vision

   b. Home Automation

   c. AI Privacy

3. Differentiate between the following: 2×2=4

   a. AI bias and AI privacy.

   b. Pros and cons of AI.

4. What do you understand by Artificial Intelligence? Write any two application of AI. 3

5. How Artificial Intelligence is used in games? 2

6. Write any two features of a Smart Home. 2

7. How is AI used in the Music and media 2

8. Write any two examples of IoT. 2

Notes

GLOSSARY

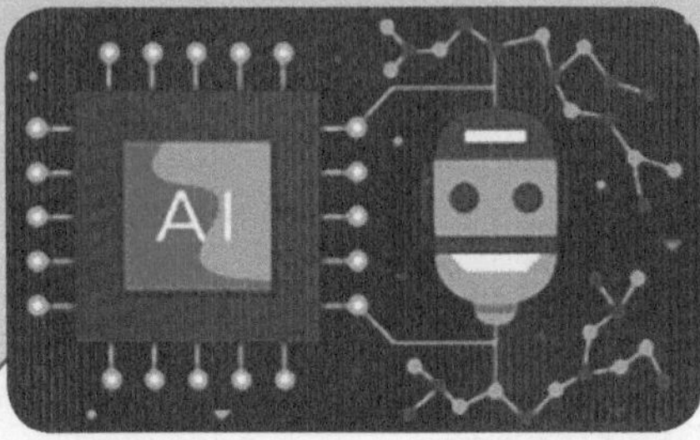

Artificial intelligence (AI): Intelligence which is demonstrated by machines, and not the natural intelligence which is shown or displayed by humans and animals.

AI Ethics: Set of values, principles, and techniques which employ widely accepted standards of right and wrong to guide moral conduct in the development and deployment of Artificial Intelligence technologies.

AI bias or Machine learning bias: Phenomenon which occurs when an algorithm produces a discriminatory result due to incorrect assumptions.

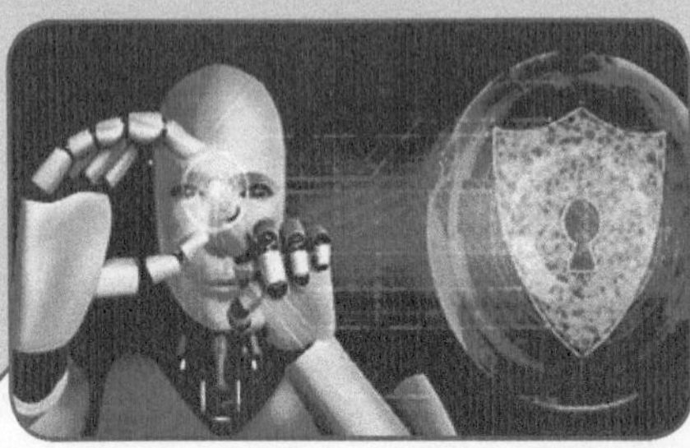

AI privacy: One's ability to control the digital data in terms of how it is stored, modified, and exchanged between the different parties.

Balloon Debate: Debate or sharing of ideas and facts among the presenters who debate to win the audience approval.

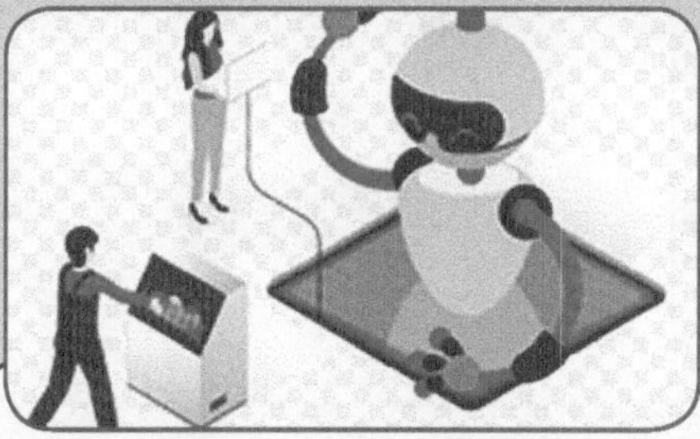

Chatbots: Software applications that use artificial intelligence & natural language processing to understand what a human wants, and guides them to their desired outcome with as little work for the end user as possible.

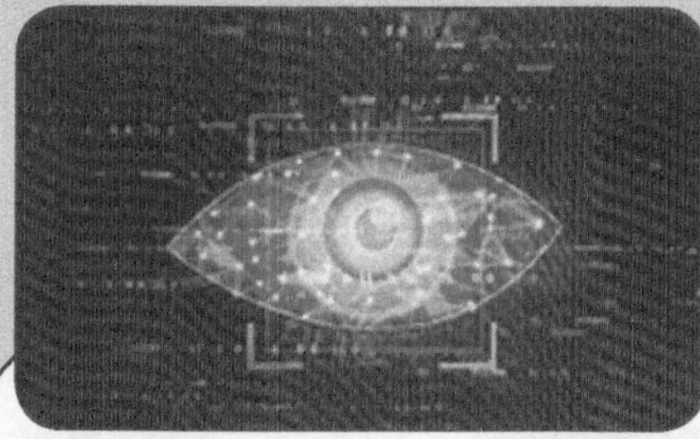

Computer vision: Interdisciplinary field that deals with how computers can be made to gain high-level understanding from digital images or videos.

Emoji Scavenger Hunt: Browser-based game built with machine learning and uses your phone's camera and a neural network to try and guess what it's seeing.

Gamification: Adding game-like components to a task to encourage the participation of user participation.

Mystery Animal: New spin on the classic 20-questions game. The computer pretends to be an animal, and you have to guess what it is using your voice. Ask any yes-or-no question you want, like "Do you have feathers?" or "Do you sleep at night?"

Natural language processing (NLP): Describes the interaction among the human language and computer.

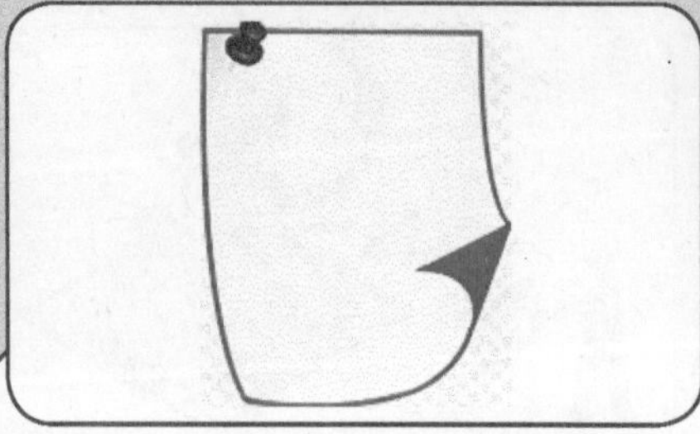

Poster: Temporary promotion of an idea, product, or event which is put up in a public space for mass consumption.

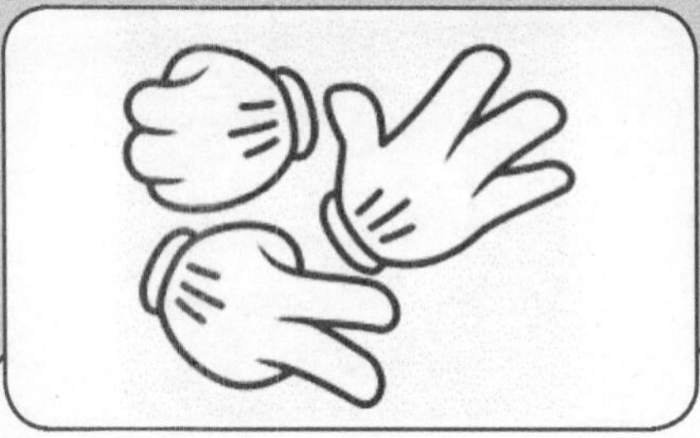

Rock paper scissors: Hand game which is played between two people, in which each player simultaneously forms one of three shapes (Rock, Paper, Scissors) with an outstretched hand.

Research: Systematic inquiry that entails collection of data, documentation of critical information, analysis and interpretation of that data/ information.

Robot ethics: Morality of how human's constructs, design, use and treat robots and other artificially intelligent created beings.

Chapterwise Solutions

Chapter 1

Brain Bot

A. 1. c 2. a 3. d 4. a 5. b

B. 1. technological 2. John McCarthy 3. Computer vision 4. machine learning 5. skills

C. 1. iv 2. i 3. v 4. ii 5. iii

Worksheet

A. 1. True 2. True 3. True 4. False 5. True

B. 1. communicating 2. three 3. Data 4. command 5. information

Quiz Card

1. c 2. a 3. a 4. c 5. d
6. b 7. a 8. d 9. a 10. a

Chapter 2

Brain Bot

A. 1. d 2. d 3. a 4. d 5. d

B. 1. collection 2. validity 3. topic 4. index cards 5. mind map

C. 1. iv 2. v 3. i 4. iii 5. ii

Worksheet

A. 1. True 2. True 3. False 4. True 5. True

B. 1. music and media 2. house temperature 3. face detection 4. Feeds 5. AI-powered bots

Quiz Card

1. c 2. a 3. b 4. b 5. c

6. a	7. a	8. c	9. c	10. c

Chapter 3

Brain Bot

A. 1. c 2. a 3. d 4. a 5. d

B. 1. AI systems 2. Robot ethics 3. Right to life 4. humans 5. cognitive tasks

C. 1. v 2. iii 3. i 4. iii 5. iv

Worksheet

A. 1. True 2. True 3. False 4. True 5. False

B. 1. ease of access 2. privacy 3. digital data 4. data-based 5. Human Intelligence

Quiz Card

1. d 2. c 3. b 4. a 5. c
6. c 7. a 8. a 9. d 10. d

Sample Paper

A. 1. b 2. c 3. d 4. d 5. a 6. b 7. d 8. a 9. a 10. a

B. 1. Technological 2. 1955 3. simulate 4. John MCarthy 5. programmed 6. Problem-solving 7. Click of button 8. gamification 9. Rock paper scissors 10. computers

C. 1. True 2. False 3. False 4. True 5. True 6. True 7. True 8. False 9. True 10. False

D. 1. iii 2. v 3. ii 4. i 5. iv
6. ix 7. vii 8. x 9. vi 10. viii

E.

1. a. Natural Language Processing
   b. Internet of Things
   c. Artificial Intelligence
2. a. Computer vision is an interdisciplinary field that deals with how computers can be made to gain high-level understanding from digital images or videos. It seeks to automate tasks that the human visual system can do.
   b. Smart homes are homes that have all the electronic devices and security systems which are controlled by the owner with the click of button.
   c. AI privacy is defined as one's ability to control the digital data in terms of how it is stored, modified, and exchanged between the different parties.
3. a. **AI bias or Machine Learning bias** is a phenomenon which occurs when an algorithm produces a discriminatory result due to incorrect assumptions.

   AI privacy is defined as one's ability to control the digital data in terms of how it is stored, modified, and exchanged between the different parties.

   b.

Advantages	Disadvantages
Reduction in Human Error (Decisions are taken from the previously gathered information by applying a certain set of algorithms. So errors are reduced and accuracy, higher degree of precision is achieved.)	High Costs of Creation (Machines repairing and maintenance cost.)
Takes risks instead of Humans (AI Robot can do the risky things for us, like going to mars, defuse a bomb, and explore the deepest parts of oceans.)	Making Humans Lazy (AI is making humans lazy with its applications automating the majority of the work.)

4. Artificial intelligence (AI) is an intelligence which is demonstrated by machines, and not the natural intelligence which is shown or displayed by humans and animals.

Applications of AI:

- **Marketing:** Marketing is a way to sugar coat your products to attract more customers, and now with AI we have an algorithm or a bot for the purpose of marketing a brand or a company. We only need to search for an item on any e-commerce store, and guess what? We get all possible results related to the item.

  Example: Finding the movies on Netflix.

- **Banking:** Banks use AI-based systems to provide customer support, detect anomalies and credit card frauds.

  Consider an example of HDFC Bank:

  Bank has developed an AI-based Chatbot called **Electronic Virtual Assistant (EVA)**, built by Bengaluru-based Senseforth AI Research.

  Eva can handle customer queries, collect knowledge from thousands of sources and provide simple answers in less than 0.4 seconds.

5. **DeepMind's AI-based AlphaGo** software, which is famous for defeating Lee Sedol, the world champion in the game of GO, is one of the most significant accomplishment in the field of AI. Other examples of Artificial Intelligence in gaming include the First Encounter Assault Recon, popularly known as F.E.A.R, which is a first-person shooter video game.
6. Two features of Smart home are:
   a. Monitor and/or control the home attributes (lighting, climate, entertainment systems)
   b. Home security (access control and alarm systems).
7. Artificial Intelligence is helping users to find music and media of their choice on apps like Spotify, Netflix, or YouTube.
8. Examples of IoT are:
   a. Connected appliances
   b. Smart home security systems